LIVING
MODERN

LIVING
MODERN

BRINGING MODERNISM HOME

andrew weaving & lisa freedman
special photography by graham atkins hughes

CHRONICLE BOOKS
SAN FRANCISCO

The Modern home as it was,

and as it is today.

BELOW The Rüthwen-Jürgensen Residence, Skodsborg,
Denmark, by Arne Jacobsen, 1956.

OPPOSITE The Bendtsen Residence, Vancouver, Canada, by
Marshall Fisher Architects and Neils Bendtsen, 2000.

First published in the United States in
2002 by Chronicle Books LLC.

Text copyright © 2001 by Quadrille
Publishing Ltd.

Page 192 constitutes a continuation of
the copyright page.

Library of Congress Cataloging-in-
Publication Data available.

ISBN 0-8118-3359-3

Printed in Singapore by Star Standard
Industries (Pte) Ltd.

Cover design by Vivien Sung

Distributed in Canada by
Raincoast Books
9050 Shaughnessy Street
Vancouver, BC V6P 6E5

10 9 8 7 6 5 4 3 2 1

Chronicle Books LLC
85 Second Street
San Francisco, California 94105

www.chroniclebooks.com

contents

foreword

OPPOSITE   The main living space, east London
BELOW   Winter Haven House, by Gene Leedy, 1956

It must be at least fifteen years since I began to put together an outline for this book. My partner and I had just created our first Modernist interior—in a mid-Victorian rowhouse in east London, of all places. Everyone we knew thought we were crazy. Why, they wondered, were we ripping out all the period features we had carefully reinstated just a few years earlier? Well, it was the only way to get a "Modern" house in London at that time. And surely there were other people out there longing for the open, uncluttered way of life we were seeking.

Soon afterward, while researching another book about the Modern Movement in the United Kingdom, I came across the first true Modernist house we would buy. It was on the Essex coast, one of a group of houses by the English architect Oliver Hill, and it was being sold by the family of the original owner, who had purchased it in 1935. Luckily it was almost unaltered. The only change was that it had all been painted white. We thought the color was original—the effect of looking at contemporary black-and-white photographs, I suppose—but in restoration we discovered that every room, and sometimes every wall in a room, was originally a different color. It turned out that our house was Oliver Hill's first show house, and he had chosen the range of colors to showcase new design and decoration. In one of his letters he said he would like to have "young Mr. Aalto's furniture" in the house. We already had a collection of Aalto pieces, so things came together quite quickly. But it was a bit like living in a museum. The conservation organization English Heritage had decided to list the house, which meant that very little could be altered. With no heating and ill-fitting steel windows, it was really comfortable for only about four weeks of the year, given the British climate.

Back in London, we decided to move closer to the heart of the city and found the ideal house. It was a blank canvas, waiting for new ideas—an early Victorian corner house that had been updated in the 1970s (avocado-colored bathroom fixtures, woodchip wallpaper, and so on), while retaining its original exterior. With no internal original features to speak of, we felt no guilt as we removed the doors and their frames and the quaint dogleg staircase. We took down walls, repositioned the staircase, and put up sliding walls and folding partitions, inspired by ideas from Le Corbusier to Richard Neutra. The project is featured in detail on pages 158–63. The whole thing seemed to evolve spontaneously. All these ideas must have been stored in my head, just waiting for the right house.

Because I am a dealer in midcentury Modern furniture and accessories, the furniture was always changing. But now we have some fairly recent work by Jasper Morrison, including tables that could trace their lineage back to Marcel Breuer, and a collection of other pieces by George Nelson, Charles and Ray Eames, and Robin Day.

On the Essex coast, a much larger Modernist house was threatened with demolition. Someone had bought it for a song with the intention of pulling it down and building a small palace in its place. Lucky for us, the local council refused the demolition. And we bought the house. It had been altered whenever there were new owners. The nautical railings had been removed, and some of the doors to terraces had been bricked up. But there were other problems, too. The (original) first-floor plan was a series of small, interconnecting rooms, and all the doors and terraces were at the front, with views of the sea but also of the road and other houses.

We reinstated all that was missing, tore down walls to create a much larger kitchen and entrance hall, and installed doors at the back of the house to give access to the garden. Inspired by all the Case Study Houses in Los Angeles, we decided to turn the integral garage into a summer living room. Full-height glass sliding doors were installed at the garden end of the new room, leading out to a pool surrounded by concrete slabs and wooden decking. Above the end of the old garage was a flat roof. Access doors were installed in the blank wall of the second-floor study, and a railing was positioned to create a terrace at the back of the house. Now the house really could be anywhere in the world. It is furnished with a range of Modernist pieces, from seating and storage from one of the Weissenhofseidlung houses to occasional furniture by Alvar Aalto and good examples of Eames and Nelson.

And now we don't seem able to stop. I looked for a small 1950s house in L.A. recently, but there was not much available, and what there was, was expensive. Then I bought a book on the Sarasota School while in Miami last year and thought "Let's have a look around there." Nothing much was coming up around Sarasota, so we decided to try a place called Winter Haven, where an architect named Gene Leedy, Paul Rudolph's first employee, had built ten houses in 1956.

Fortunately he still lived in one of them, and in tracking him down, we discovered that he had an option to buy the house opposite for a good price. An elderly lady had lived there for years, and even though things had been added, nothing had been taken away, except the jalousie windows. We bought it without viewing—a bit of a risk, but worth it. Our first visit was quite a shock, though. The floors were covered with pink shag-pile carpet, and the kitchen cabinets with wood-effect Fablon. We spent our first week just clearing out rubbish and additions. But the house was basically in good shape—we found the original cork flooring under the carpets and great-condition wooden cabinets under the Fablon. The house is now a wonderful example of the Sarasota School, furnished with furniture of the 1950s, and a part of the story of Modernism just beginning to be acknowledged internationally.

BELOW AND OPPOSITE   The house on the Essex coast

Introducing **Living Modern**

Fifteen years later, my interest in Modernism is as great as ever. But how the world has changed. Now it seems that with every year, more and more people want to live in a contemporary way in newly built or newly renovated homes. And so now that we have infinitely more personal experience to call on, that initial outline—for an accessible, inspiring book about Modernism—is finding its audience.

The first section, BIRTH OF MODERN, explores the history of Modernism. It describes the "birth" of this extraordinary design revolution and tells how the Modern Movement swept the world, expanding from its twin epicenters in western Europe and California to influence architectural and design styles around the world.

CLASSIC MODERN, the second section, showcases thirteen significant Modern houses, most of which can still be seen in close to their original states. I chose them to indicate just how innovative and diverse the pioneering works of the movement were and to demonstrate the vision of modern living that lies behind the term "Modernism", as well as the architectural ideals.

MODERN TRADEMARKS focuses on architects and designers discussed in the first two sections, highlighting anything from their signature use of color, materials, or lighting to their placing of furniture to pinpoint, for the aspiring Modernist, features that can be incorporated in the interiors of today.

MODERN NOW shows a selection of contemporary interiors that follow in the tradition of the classics. Some are Modern interiors created in pre-Modern buildings, others are new builds, and others are totally remodeled originals. To encourage and inspire, I have chosen to include the work of talented amateurs, as well as that of leading architects and interior designers, because whether you own a Victorian row house, a high-rise apartment, a shingle-roofed bungalow, or a suburban tract house, Modern living can be yours.

The origins of Modernism are as tangled and debated as the causes of its near contemporary, World War I. Yet nearly a hundred years since its beginnings, at the turn of the twentieth century, it is clear that Modernism has become one of the great architectural styles, continuing to influence the way we design and live in our homes today.

Modernism is rooted in an attempt to create an architecture for a new machine age, for a time when innovations in materials and building techniques allowed a flexibility of design undreamed of in millennia of bricks and mortar.

There was also a strong moral and philosophical basis to the work of many of the early Modernists: a conscious wish to express in three dimensions the political, social, and economic theories being advanced by contemporary writers and thinkers. They believed that by transforming architecture, they could transform society itself, making the way we live healthier and more stable.

But beyond its social message and enthusiasm for machines and their products, Modernism had various clear imperatives: in particular, an emphasis on light, openness, and honesty. And this aesthetic credo has been its greatest legacy to succeeding generations.

Modernism flowered as a design theory after World War I, but its roots lay in the mid-nineteenth century, when the Arts and Crafts Movement began the campaign to simplify architecture and the interior. William Morris and his followers campaigned against the clutter, fussiness, and sheer gloominess of Victorian design, advocating in their stead "total environments", in which furniture, applied decoration, and wall surfaces could work together to create harmony, simplicity, and light.

The great technical advances of the nineteenth century—in particular, new materials such as steel and reinforced concrete—were also, of course, fundamental steps on the road to Modernism, for without these innovations the flexible interior walls and large expanses of window that characterize the style would never have been achievable. And with these innovations, too, came the call for a machine aesthetic, one that would reveal rather than obscure the products of the factory and the engineer.

As early as 1896, the Viennese architect **Otto Wagner** predicted an architecture of "horizontal lines . . . and great simplicity." His fellow Austrian **Adolf Loos** published in 1908 his famous essay "Ornament and Crime", in which he equated decoration with decadence and criminality. The latter's early-twentieth-century buildings—such as the reinforced-concrete Steiner Residence (1911) in Vienna—predated by some ten years the stripped aesthetic of the Modern Movement.

But Modernism had equally strong roots on the other side of the Atlantic, where America's greatest architect, **Frank Lloyd Wright**, had begun to revolutionize the structure of the house itself.

Wright's Prairie houses, designed between 1894 and 1910 for wealthy Chicago suburbanites, were a startling and influential departure, with their long, low profiles, rooms running into each other, terraces merging with gardens, and projecting roofs. These elements of his work would be taken further by his European followers, but Wright was never to confine himself to what became the Modernist aesthetic.

The Meyer May Residence, Grand Rapids, Michigan by Frank Lloyd Wright, 1908.
Wright's Prairie houses, with their low-pitched, almost Japanese, roofs, set at varying
levels over an elongated, asymmetrical plan, were to influence architects worldwide.
No one in the first decade of the twentieth century came as near as Wright to the
style that became known as Modernism.

ABOVE LEFT Rudolf Schindler (right) with Richard and Dionne Neutra and their son Dion at the King's Road House in 1928. The two pioneering Viennese architects and their families shared the house for several years from the mid-1920s.

ABOVE RIGHT The interior of the King's Road House, Los Angeles, by Rudolf Schindler and Clyde Chase, 1920–21. Chase, an engineer, and his wife lived here with the Schindlers until the mid-1920s. The house was groundbreaking in its informality, its minimal interiors, its elemental furnishings, and its linking of the house with nature.

The movement that was to become known in the 1930s as the International Style really came fully into being after World War I, both in the United States and in Europe. In America, two young Viennese architects, Rudolf Schindler and Richard J. Neutra, who had both been briefly employed by Wright in Chicago and then in Los Angeles, were among the first to integrate revolutionary architectural ideas from Europe with Wright's notions of the modern to create some of the most exciting private housing of the first three decades of the century.

In 1921 **Rudolf Schindler,** who had worked with Wright in Los Angeles on his famed Hollyhock House, built a house for himself on King's Road, Los Angeles. Its minimal interiors, concrete floors, cool open spaces, and integration of the natural world outside and the man-made interior were to remain influential throughout the twentieth century.

By the time he died in 1953, Schindler had designed over 500 buildings, more than 150 of which—mainly family houses—had been built. Throughout his career he concentrated on using inexpensive, mass-produced materials and, finding imaginative solutions to individual demands. It was, however, his willingness to work within tight budgets and accommodate himself to the needs of his clients that excluded him throughout his lifetime from the prescriptive world of the Modernist avant-garde. Ironically, it is these very qualities that today are so prized in his work.

Schindler's fellow countryman—and for several years housemate—**Richard Neutra** had an even more profound influence on early Modernism as it developed in the United States. Neutra had studied with Adolf Loos in Vienna before arriving in Chicago in 1923 to work with Frank Lloyd Wright.

Eventually Neutra set up his own practice on the West Coast; and with his Lovell Health House of 1927–29, designed for the health journalist and guru Dr. Philip Lovell, he was among the first on either side of the Atlantic to use a steel skeleton and standardized factory components, including casements and glass and metal panels, in domestic architecture. The house was radical, too, in the pioneering way it embraced the newly evolving California lifestyle, blurring the boundaries between indoors and out.

Neutra became one of the leading exponents of Modernism in the United States. His work remained largely domestic (pp. 74–7 and 104–5), and his strength continued to be his exceptional ability to site a house in landscape, a talent he demonstrated outstandingly in his own house at Silver Lake (1933), Los Angeles, as well as in such later works as the Miller Residence (1936), Palm Springs; the Desert House (1946), Colorado; and the Kaufmann Residence (1947), Palm Springs.

Indeed, it is the relationship of structure to nature that is key to the work of Schindler and Neutra. Both considered that it was the architect's responsibility to nurture that relationship by the careful consideration of the site, the skillful manipulation of daylight and sunlight, and the imaginative use of landscaping.

American Modernism, however, was to remain the softer face of the new movement. The sunny West Coast, untroubled by the devastation of World War I, had the freedom to interpret Modernism as a technically and aesthetically innovative style, but it was a style that would continue to be, for the time being at least, the preserve of the indulged, if enlightened, rich.

The Lovell Health House, Los Angeles, by Richard Neutra, 1927–29, was to epitomize the relationship between the new forms in design and the new healthy modern lifestyle. Beautifully situated on an idyllic site, this house, with its steel-frame skeleton and lightweight synthetic skin, would later be considered to sum up the International Style's ideal of a clean, white, open architecture.

The rise of Nazism killed the Bauhaus. Walter Gropius and Marcel Breuer left Germany, first for Britain and then for the United States. Their arrival in the States in the late 1930s had an enormous impact on American architecture and design. This photograph shows the Breuers' house in Lincoln, Massachusetts, 1938–39, built by Walter Gropius. (For Gropius's own house in Lincoln, see pp. 44–7). Marcel Breuer is holding the camera on the right, Gropius is at far left, the blonde on the right is Gropius's wife, Ise. The Short chairs, nesting tables and sofa are by Breuer, part of the range designed for Jack Pritchard of Isokon while Breuer was in Britain (p. 99).

LEFT Marcel Breuer (far left), his wife, Max Plant (unknown), Frank Lloyd Wright, and Walter Gropius, on the terrace of Gropius's home (p. 44) in Lincoln, Massachusetts, 1940.

Postwar European architects viewed their role somewhat differently. Profoundly affected by the devastation of the war they had just experienced, they wished to create a new world in all forms of art and design. And it was here, in Europe, that the early work of three outstanding architects—Walter Gropius, Ludwig Mies van der Rohe, and Le Corbusier—would lay the foundations of Modernism's worldwide influence.

In 1919 **Walter Gropius** was appointed director of the amalgamated state schools of fine art and craft in the German city of Weimar. Named the Bauhaus by Gropius himself, the title suggested the medieval *bauhütte* (or stonemasons' lodge), an indication that Gropius intended to create a classless guild of artists and craftsmen. The school was to pursue a new approach to design education, becoming, in spite of its short life, the most famous design school of the twentieth century. Gropius introduced a syllabus that would equip students with the skills necessary for the new industrial society, and the young men and women who arrived at the Bauhaus believed that they were, in the words of Walter Gropius, "starting from zero."

Though influenced by the Arts and Crafts Movement and also by the work of Frank Lloyd Wright, Gropius believed that the Bauhaus should concentrate on the design of objects for mass production. He also believed that because the new architecture was being created for the mass of workers, it needed to reject elements of design traditionally associated with the ruling classes. So, decorative pitched roofs and ornate cornices—distinguishing characteristics of the old architecture of the nobility—were replaced by flat roofs and sheer façades, while ostentatious materials, such as granite, marble, limestone, and labor-intensive architectural ornament, were all deemed inappropriate.

In their place, Bauhaus architecture introduced the idea of "expressed structure". Since technically it was no longer necessary for a structure to be supported by its walls—frames of steel and reinforced concrete now did that—it was considered "dishonest" to make walls look as though they were in fact loadbearing. They were to become thin skins that did nothing to conceal the way in which a building had been created. The basic structure of the building—with its machine-made parts—should be clearly visible from the outside.

Bauhaus interiors were stripped bare and painted white. They had open floor plans, curtailing the old individualistic, bourgeois obsession with privacy. And they excluded ornamental wallpaper, carpeting, draperies, and decorative detailing, such as cornices and rails. Chintz chair upholstery and decorative fabrics were also rejected. Instead, furniture was made of "honest" materials, such as leather, tubular steel, bentwood, cane, and canvas. Rugs and carpets were supplanted by concrete, linoleum, and wood.

For Bauhaus designers, furniture offered even greater potential for experimentation than architecture. A large-scale industry of mass-produced furniture had been in existence since the beginning of the twentieth century, but production methods were still essentially reliant on traditional design. There was no commercially available furniture that could be successfully integrated into the new living spaces. And leading members of the Bauhaus, such as ex-student **Marcel Breuer,** began to produce furniture better suited to the new Machine Age. The streamlined, sculptural, and continuous lines of Breuer's tubular-steel cantilevered chair—the Cesca Chair, B32—became the perfect small-scale expression of modernity.

ABOVE The director's office in the Bauhaus, Weimar, Germany, 1923. Gropius had become director in 1919, and he was to inspire its artists and architects to work together to create "the building of the future." All the furniture was designed by Gropius. The wall hangings and rugs are from Bauhaus craft studios and reflect the influence of Paul Klee. The light fixtures are inspired by industrial models. This photograph was used to publicize a exhibition that Gropius organized in 1923. The school moved to custom-built premises in Dessau in 1926.

RIGHT Le Corbusier's apartment in the rue Nungesser et Coli, near the Bois de Bologne, Paris, France. He lived and worked here for many years. The barrel-vaulted open-plan living space and other domestic quarters were smooth, painted plaster. His studio was rough brick. The small table in the foreground—a cross section from a tree trunk, polished and fitted with metal legs—is by Charlotte Perriand, while the Grand Confort armchair is a collaboration by Perriand, Le Corbusier, and his cousin Pierre Jeanneret. The bentwood dining chairs are by Thonet and typical of those he placed in all his early houses. The vertical, full-length louvres at the window, apparently made of wood, are not typical of Corbusier's work.

ABOVE Villa Church, Ville d'Avray, France, by Le Corbusier, 1927–29. Designed for a couple of expatriate Americans, the Villa Church is one of the earliest of a series of houses Le Corbusier built for wealthy clients in the late 1920s and early 1930s (see also pp. 40–43). Uncharacteristically, much of the furniture is credited to Charlotte Perriand alone. The metal-and-leather chairs, first exhibited in 1928, were both metaphorically and literally revolutionary as the backs could be swung in a complete circle. Two of the matching stools are also visible. The tabletop was made of glass (by Saint-Gobain), set on a metal base, and another with a golden glass top was made for the library.

Gropius and his contemporaries were able to demonstrate to the mass of the German public what Bauhaus theory could produce at a worker-housing exhibition held in Stuttgart in 1927. Under the architectural direction of **Ludwig Mies van der Rohe,** the creation of the Weissenhofsiedlung exhibition brought together Modernist architects from all over Europe to build model city dwellings on new lines. With these light and airy houses and apartment blocks the young revolutionaries of the movement were able to show just how appealing low-cost urban housing could be.

The Swiss-born architect **Le Corbusier** (pseudonym of Charles-Édouard Jeanneret), arguably the most influential and brilliant of all twentieth-century architects, was largely responsible for making the world aware that a new style had been born. Though initially trained in Switzerland as a designer-engraver, Le Corbusier traveled widely in Europe during the formative years of his study of architecture (from 1907 to 1916) and was also aware of the work of Frank Lloyd Wright.

He set up his practice in Paris in 1916 and dedicated himself to establishing a new aesthetic for a new way of life. His chief source of inspiration was the machine – he expressed it in his much-quoted aphorism "The house is a machine for living." He wanted to create an architecture that functioned with the same efficiency as a car.

By the early 1920s Le Corbusier had begun to create new types of housing. Versions of his Maison Citrohan, first conceived in 1920 and exhibited at the Salon d'Automne in Paris in 1922, with their asymmetric plans, large window areas, and terraces made possible by the use of reinforced concrete, expressed the spirit of change more clearly than anything that had yet been designed.

But Le Corbusier's influence lay as much in his published work as in the buildings he designed. (As the architectural historian Henry-Russell Hitchcock has it, "He crystallized; he dramatized but he was not alone in creating.") The vigorous propaganda he contributed to the magazine *L'Esprit Nouveau* between 1920 and 1925 and the books he wrote subsequently, exploring his vision of the future, have dominated the philosophy of Modernist architecture.

In 1923 Le Corbusier published the seminal work *Vers une Architecture*, and in 1926 he outlined *Les Cinq Points d'une Architecture Nouvelle*. These five points—the *pilotis* (or columns) that raised the mass of a house off the ground; the free plan, which was achieved by separating the loadbearing columns from the walls subdividing the space; the free façade, now a thin, independent, nonstructural membrane, which could be punctuated at will by windows and doors; the long, horizontal sliding window (or *fenêtre en longueur*); and the roof garden, which in theory restored the area of ground covered by the house—were to become the ABC of the Modern Movement.

In 1925 Le Corbusier's Pavilion de L'Esprit Nouveau was the sensation of the Exposition Internationale des Arts Decoratifs et Industriels Modernes in Paris. This strikingly modern design adapted his earlier Maison Citrohan as a living unit for high-density dwellings. Constructed using standardized parts, it had an interior space that was entirely free in plan. Solid walls were removed, and distinct living areas were created by pieces of furniture or sliding screens.

In the following few years, in a series of modern villas for wealthy clients in the Paris suburbs, including the Villa Stein at Garches (1926–27) and the Villa Savoye at Poissy (1928–31, pp. 40–3 and 96), Le Corbusier was to refine his principles to much-admired and much-copied levels of mastery.

At the same period—because he believed that Modern machines demanded modern *équipement d'habitation* (equipment for living)—Le Corbusier collaborated with the French furniture designer **Charlotte Perriand** to produce a furniture range in tubular steel and leather, first shown at the Salon d'Automne in Paris in 1929. These pieces—the Grand Confort armchair and the Chaise Longue—have become classics of Modern design.

From the early 1930s onward, however, Le Corbusier began to turn away from the glass-and-metal purity of his machine-aesthetic designs. In its place he developed an antirational, textured, sculptural style—seen in such buildings as the Unité d'Habitation (1952) in Marseilles and the Maisons Jaoul (1951–55, pp. 60–3) in Paris—which ultimately became as influential as his more schematic earlier work.

L'Unité d'Habitation, Marseilles, France, by Le Corbusier, 1952. Designed as social housing for the poor, this vast apartment block, finished in rough-textured concrete and raised on its massive *pilotis*, has become an icon of the Modern Movement. Its 337 apartments on seventeen floors were served by a shopping arcade, hotel, roof deck, running track, kindergarten, paddling pool, and gym—a complete city in one building, hence the name. Individual apartments, with their double-height ceilings and concrete walls, were surprisingly comfortable and quiet and have now been comprehensively colonized by the middle classes.

ABOVE The Farnsworth Residence, Plano, Illinois, by Mies van der Rohe (1946–51), is the perfect Miesian glass box. A light, transparent, seemingly weightless pavilion, floating between floor and ceiling slabs, it is subdivided only by an elongated service core and carefully positioned furniture designed by Mies himself.

OPPOSITE The Lake Shore Drive Apartments, Chicago, Illinois, by Mies van der Rohe, 1951. In the austere, elegant, geometric blocks of these soaring metal-frame apartments, Mies reinterpreted his Weissenhofsiedlung apartment designs of 1927 (p. 21). Here, each apartment is entered through a service core, consisting of kitchen and bathrooms, while the living space, apportioned according to the size of the unit, runs around the perimeter.

Ludwig Mies van der Rohe advanced toward the new style less rapidly than Le Corbusier or his fellow countryman Gropius. However, in his design project for a country house in 1922, he had already broken with the concept of the wall as a continuous plane surrounding the plan, achieving a greater openness than even Le Corbusier.

In the early 1920s Mies had also become preoccupied with the reflective qualities of glass, seeing it as a material whose surface could be subject to constant transformation under the impact of light. "I discovered," Mies wrote in 1921, "by working with actual glass models, that the important thing is the play of reflections and not the effect of light and shadow as in ordinary buildings."

Though Mies had absorbed the German Neoclassical tradition, he was also influenced in his use of horizontal profiles extending into landscape by the Prairie houses of Frank Lloyd Wright. He took both a step further in the revolutionary single-story building he designed as the German Pavilion for the Barcelona exhibition of 1929 (pp. 96–7). Here, in the first of his templelike structures, Mies brought Neoclassicism up to date. Between eight freestanding columns supporting a flat roof, he slid flat planes of plate glass and polished marble, to create an elegantly simple structure. Its open plan and masterly spatial composition, its use of precious materials, its technically perfect finish, and its introduction of his seminal, steel-framed Barcelona Chair were to make it hugely influential throughout the twentieth century.

The Bauhaus was already under attack when Mies accepted its directorship in 1930. The Nazis had, right from the start, perceived the white walls, steel windows, and flat roofs of Modernist architecture as an internationalist ideology proposed by an intellectual elite with socialist sympathies. Mies announced the dissolution of the faculty after police and storm troopers closed the building in 1933, three months after Hitler's accession to power.

After 1933 nothing by Mies was built in Germany, but during a working trip to the United States in 1937 he accepted an offer to become Professor of Architecture at the Armour Institute (now the Illinois Institute) of Technology in Chicago—a move that was to bring him a wide and wealthy following in the States.

His post–World War II work demonstrated his austere yet elegant application of many of the principles evolved during the 1920s in Germany. His famous aphorism "Less is more"—reflecting his ability to derive maximum effect from a minimal use of form—sums up an approach that later became widely known as minimalism and was of profound significance in shaping the urban landscape of postwar America.

Even greater was his contribution to the development of the American skyscraper. In such perfectly executed buildings as the Lake Shore Drive Apartments in Chicago (1951), he was able to express in glass and steel the ambition and spirit of the most powerful nation in the world, while his bronze-clad Seagram Building (1958), built in collaboration with Philip Johnson in New York for the Canadian distiller, was to become a symbol of the hierarchical structure of American executive life, inspiring hundreds of replicas throughout the world.

The Frinton Park Estate, Frinton, Essex, England, 1934–37. Oliver Hill was the mastermind behind the plan to build an estate of Modernist houses and public buildings at the then fashionable east-coast seaside resort. Some of the country's leading interpreters of Modernism participated in the project but the development faltered and the public buildings were never built. Frinton, however, still has the largest group of Modernist houses in Britain. Oliver Hill's designs for Frinton were primarily concerned with capturing the external features of Modernism. The plan of his houses was essentially Edwardian, designed for a middle-class clientele who wanted the gloss of the new lifestyle and the reassurance of the old. Apart from a large living room with recessed dining room, the ground floor was subdivided into a series of small rooms, including spaces for a live-in maid and for hats and coats.

While the giants of early Modernist architecture on the Continent were exploring their own particular visions in the '20s, the new style had only the slightest influence in Britain. But by the mid-1930s Britain had become one of the few countries where, for political reasons, Modern architects could practice at all, and London was the first stop for many architects fleeing the rise of National Socialism in Germany.

It was fortunate that they had not arrived in the previous decade. In the 1920s they would have found a wide range of fashionable "modern" styles, ranging from Beaux-Arts classicism to the soulless ornament of Art Deco, but none of them was Modernist. "A French exponent of Modernism has built a plate-glass box to form one of these new abodes—one could not conceive it as a home for anyone save a vegetarian bacteriologist," commented the president of the Architectural Association, Gilbert Jenkins, during his annual address in London in 1927. The "French exponent" he was referring to was Le Corbusier, and the house was one of two he built for the Weissenhofsiedlung exhibition.

By 1930, however, a younger group of architects had founded the 20th Century Group, with the intention of starting a "pure, modern movement in English architecture", and by the time that F. R. S. Yorke published his book *The Modern House* in 1934, there was already a significant body of "pure" buildings in Britain to record.

Yorke belonged to a small and exclusive circle of largely émigré architects that included the Canadian Wells Coates, the Russian Berthold Lubetkin and the Swede Ove Arup. Together, in 1933, they founded the MARS group (Modern Architectural Research Society), whose mission was to introduce Continental Modernism to Britain.

New money in Britain had traditionally sought social acceptability by ownership of a Georgian or Victorian estate in the country, but now there were those who could see that the white Modernist villa, with its streamlined appearance and efficient interior, was well suited to such status symbols as the automobile and the vacuum cleaner.

Oliver Hill was a country-house architect who, in the 1930s, abandoned his earlier enthusiasm for Edwin Lutyens to cater to this clientele. He became established both as a successful exponent of the style in his villas—Joldwynds (Holmbury St. Mary in Surrey, 1933), Holthanger (Wentworth in Surrey, 1933–35), Landfall (Poole in Dorset, 1936–38), and Hill House (Redington Road in north London's Hampstead, 1936–38); but more significant still was his influence on the taste of the patrons themselves and his own patronage of such younger architects as Wells Coates and the Connell, Ward, and Lucas partnership in the Frinton Park Estate project in Essex (1934–37).

Wells Coates's first major work was the Isokon apartment block at Lawn Road in north London's Hampstead, built in 1933. These short-lease studio apartments, built from reinforced concrete, were designed for a new generation of highly mobile intellectuals and artists. They were notable as an attempt to establish a Modern way of life—austere, motorized and peripatetic—beyond the confines of the standard city flat and the suburban duplex.

The most inventive partnership in Britain specializing in house design was **Connell, Ward, and Lucas,** and the most assured work of these two New Zealanders and an Englishman was the house they designed in Frognal, in Hampstead. This reinforced-concrete villa, built in 1938, employed such Corbusier-inspired motifs as a first floor partly raised on *pilotis*; a garage under the house; an open sundeck on the roof; long, strip windows; and full-length glass doors, which slid away to let the city dweller enjoy the greenery and light outside. Like Le Corbusier's Villa Stein before it, this house suggested a radical new direction for urban living.

By the time Gropius and Breuer arrived in Britain, on their way to the United States, they were able to provide a rich injection of enthusiasm to a movement that already had its own momentum, gaining impetus from such other Continental modernizers as the great Finnish architect and designer Alvar Aalto (p. 30), whose inexpensive, mass-produced bent-plywood furniture had already become standard in many British homes—modern or otherwise.

Nonetheless, while by 1939 the amount of work being produced in the new style showed that it had gained a foothold in the national aesthetic consciousness, Modern architecture remained to many British people an anomaly—cold, austere, and foreign. And it was really only in the 1990s that the ideas of these early Modernists found a wider audience in British homes.

LEFT The Isokon apartments, London, England, 1933, by Wells Coates, were a milestone in the introduction of the Modernist idiom to Britain. The four-story reinforced concrete block, planned with twenty-two "minimum" flats for single people, offered a new lifestyle to the intellectual bohemian. The residents' club became a fashionable meeting place for Bauhaus exiles such as Walter Gropius and Marcel Breuer.

BELOW The interior of Connell, Ward, and Lucas's Corbusier-inspired villa in London's Hampstead, England, 1938. Following Corbusier's 1920s villas, the main living space is on the first floor, opening onto a terrace with a stairway leading to the garden.

Modernism ran to a different timetable, too, in the United States. The Modern Movement—as a coherently expressed idea—was introduced to America in an exhibition at the Museum of Modern Art in New York in 1932, entitled "Modern Architecture: International Exhibition". Under the curatorship of the museum's director, Alfred Barr, the head of the Department of Architecture and Design, Philip Johnson, and the architectural historian Henry-Russell Hitchcock, this enormously influential exhibition prepared the ground for the arrival of Walter Gropius, Ludwig Mies van der Rohe, and Marcel Breuer at the end of the 1930s, and was decisive in the impact they would have on academia and on the profession at large.

But Modernism was never to have the same resonance in the States as it had in Europe. In Europe, it was part of a cultural and artistic revolution, often deeply interwoven with political polemic. On the other side of the Atlantic, it continued to operate free of political overtones, liberating both its European exponents—who produced an energetic body of work in America—and its native practitioners.

Ironically, Frank Lloyd Wright was not one of Modernism's champions. From the 1920s onward, he had gone more and more his own way (pp. 38–9 and 93). One exception in his work, however, is Fallingwater (1935–37), in Bear Run, Pennsylvania, which was built as a retreat for the department-store owner Edgar Kaufmann. The house, with its central core of concrete, timber, steel, and glass and its cantilevered concrete balconies (p. 92), is formally within the Modernist aesthetic. But its powerful combination of man-made and natural forms and its intensely emotional integration of building with the landscape and water that surround it, testify that Wright, even at his most International, remains more closely linked to the Romantic tradition.

Philip Johnson, the son of a wealthy New England family, was to remain the most influential early advocate of European Modernist ideas in the States. A witty, urbane character, he had studied philology at Harvard before joining the Museum of Modern Art in 1930. In the early 1940s he trained under Gropius and Breuer at Harvard, and in 1949 he built his own Mies-inspired Glass House in the woods at New Canaan, Connecticut. An exquisite steel-section cube encased in sheet glass, it remains one of the best examples of Modern Movement design and

The Glass House, by Philip Johnson, New Canaan, Connecticut, 1949.
A leading disseminator of Modern Movement ideas in America, Philip Johnson, became (briefly) one of its dazzling exponents. His most famous essay in the style, this building in the woods of Connecticut, derives from Mies van der Rohe's plate-glass pavilions, in particular the Farnsworth Residence (p. 22). But while Mies extended the horizontal plane indefinitely with his great floor and ceiling slabs, the focus in Johnson's design is the brick cylinder that pierces the roof, creating a more sculptural effect.

The radical design for the Fairchild Residence (New York, 1941), by George Nelson and William Hamby, was the cover story for the April 1943 issue of *Fortune* magazine (see pp. 54–57).

propaganda. It was, however, a commitment he was unable to sustain. His later work was much more varied and unexpected, moving into early post-Modernism in the 1960s with such works as the New York State Theatre (1962–64), at the Lincoln Center for the Performing Arts.

In the mid-1940s **George Nelson** was co-managing editor of *Architectural Forum* and a significant figure in American Modernism. In 1945 he and his fellow editor Henry Wright produced the seminal book *Tomorrow's House*. Nelson had studied architecture at Yale in the 1930s, and then followed two years in Italy, where he interviewed many of the leading figures of the Modern Movement, among them Gropius. Practicing only sporadically as an architect, Nelson produced several innovative designs, including his 1941 masterpiece, the Fairchild Residence.

But it was in the new profession of industrial design that Nelson has had the most enduring impact. In 1946 he began a long association with the United States's most prestigious furniture company, Herman Miller. Here, as director of design, he developed his Action office system, introducing the idea of storage panels as space dividers. Widely adopted in the 1960s, it was to revolutionize office space by helping to create more flexible working environments. Nelson's design office also produced some of the twentieth century's canonical pieces, including the ball clock, the bubble lamp, and the sling sofa, many of which are still in production.

Paul Rudolph was another Gropius pupil who was to have an enormous impact on the American architectural scene. A preacher's son from Alabama, Rudolph first studied architecture in Alabama before going on to the graduate program at Harvard, under Gropius and Breuer. By the age of forty—young for an architect—he had attracted attention for a series of light, elegant schools and houses in the Sarasota area in Florida (pp. 12–13).

After his appointment as chairman of Yale's Architecture School in 1958, Rudolph enjoyed a meteoric rise, wielding extraordinary influence both on his own students and on young architects around the world. As one critic said of him, "Here was the second generation of Gropius that was going to remake the world." In the post-Modernist 1960s, however, the uncompromising Rudolph went badly out of fashion, and he worked largely in urban planning and in Asia. It is only recently that his work has begun to be reevaluated as the so-called Sarasota School is recognized.

ABOVE *Arts & Architecture* magazine, March 1947. Publisher John Entenza used the magazine to promote his California-based Case Study House Program, intended to "lead the house out of the bondage of handcraftism into industry."

And Gropius's influence was to travel well beyond Europe and the United States. One of his most talented Harvard students was the Viennese-born, Canadian-educated **Harry Seidler,** who had traveled on a scholarship to study under the great master in 1945–46. Seidler then worked briefly for Breuer in New York before joining his refugee parents in Australia, a country ripe for the introduction of Modernist architecture.

"Gropius instilled in us," Seidler later recalled, "a certain conscience in order that his students did not do "unreasonable things", physically or aesthetically … he taught us to create socially responsible architecture." Seidler imported both the notion of a socially responsible architecture and the Bauhaus white box to Australia, a land where the architecture of "sun, light and air" could be far more effectively deployed than it had been in its chilly northern homeland (pp. 58–9).

Meanwhile in the United States, Modernism continued to flourish independently, outside the Harvard axis, on the West Coast—above all in the houses designed and built under the directive of John Entenza's Case Study House Program. In 1937 Entenza purchased and became the editor of an obscure California magazine, which he renamed *Arts & Architecture*. Between 1945 and 1962 he used the magazine to showcase a series of experimental houses designed by some of California's leading architects, including Richard Neutra, Raphael Soriano, Charles Eames, Craig Ellwood, and Pierre Koenig.

The Case Study House Program houses were intended to be the prototypes of good mass housing in response to postwar shortages in housing and materials. They were also to be constructed from simple, mass-produced, standardized factory products that were readily and cheaply available. And they offered a model of modern living. Unlike many of the individual villas created in the Modernist style in Europe, which were, in fact, houses for the rich, these buildings

showed architects concentrating for the first time on small, single-family dwellings for the average American household. With their open-plan interiors, carports, carefully chosen sites, and generous and well-landscaped gardens, they remain an idealized vision of the California way of life.

Charles Eames was best known as a furniture designer, but his fascination with new technology was to extend beyond chairs into structures. No. 8, the house he and his wife, Ray, designed for the Case Study House Program in 1949 in Los Angeles, consists of two steel-framed prefabricated units bought from an industrial catalog (see also pp. 102–3). Its radical departure from the European Modernist tradition was its introduction of color. The frame was painted black and filled with a mosaic of opaque materials, some painted in bright yellow, red, and blue.

Pierre Koenig was a slightly younger architect. From the start of his career he was deeply committed to prefabrication and the new technology of the postwar world. He designed and built his first exposed-steel house in 1950 while still a student, proving that the use of prefabricated materials could allow for spatial freedom in affordable housing. In 1957 he was chosen by Entenza to design Case Study Houses Nos. 21 and 22 (pp. 66–69 and 106–7).

Koenig's houses were showcases of contemporary building technology, domestic design, furniture, and fixtures. Each house is premised on the idea of ease and accessibility, and Koenig makes extensive use of glass to extend outdoor space visually into the interior. The kitchens, too, fitted with the latest in refrigeration technology, were turned around so that meals could be served directly outdoors. At the same time, open planning of the space indoors—furnished with the latest plastic and steel-framed furniture—allowed work and play to be carried out in one space rather than in individual rooms. These two stylish and sophisticated houses demonstrated to an enthusiastic audience just how relaxed and easy Modern living could be.

ABOVE Case Study House No. 21 in construction, 1957. California-born Pierre Koenig was a latecomer to the Program, but his passion for steel-frame construction and his youthful empathy with the postwar world enabled him to create one of its most strikingly contemporary statements.

OPPOSITE TOP Case Study House No. 8, Pacific Palisades, Los Angeles, by Charles and Ray Eames, 1949. True to Entenza's dictum that modern housing should employ ready-made industrial components, the Eames House was constructed using a lightweight steel frame, infilled with glass panels. Viewed from the gallery, the architects sit in their double-height living room on and among their own-design furniture and eclectic collection of ethnic pieces.

Gradually, after World War II, architects began a general process of reworking prewar Modernism in an attempt to engage with the new consumer society, science, technology, and the Space Age. From the 1950s there had been demands that Modern architecture should become less rigid, and one of the most significant results was the dominance during this decade of Scandinavian design, with its far gentler approach to form and materials.

The great Scandinavian architect **Alvar Aalto,** though indebted to his Modern Movement contemporaries farther south, had been incorporating traditional techniques and local building materials in his design since the 1930s. By the end of World War II, he had evolved a language entirely his own, which, with its vigorous display of curved walls and single pitched roofs and use of timber and brick, was entirely in harmony with the international trend toward more expressive design.

Aalto's lifelong attempt to satisfy social and psychological criteria effectively set him apart from the more dogmatic functionalists of the 1920s. He focused on creating an environment that would be conducive to human well-being, and his work, while rejecting some of the purist geometric tradition, also gained in warmth, richness, and feeling (pp. 100–1).

However, Aalto's significance lies not only in his buildings but in his product design, which he always saw as an essential component of his architecture. His bent-plywood furniture and his famous stacking stool, both developed during the 1930s, are perhaps his most classic pieces, revealing his regard for practicality, his characteristic sensitivity to linear elegance, and his profound feeling for organic forms and textures. His period as visiting Professor of Architecture at the Massachusetts Institute of Technology in 1946–47 can only have strengthened his already profound influence on Modern design.

Another Scandinavian architect to fuse his local tradition with that of mainstream Modernism was the Dane **Arne Jacobsen.** In common with many Scandinavian architects of his generation, Jacobsen concerned himself with every aspect of a building's design, paying as much attention to the interior and the fixtures as to the structure (pp. 64–5 and 112–13).

Though most of Jacobsen's designs for silverware, textiles, and furniture were created for specific projects, they had an immediate appeal to a wider audience, and many have become classics. His Ant Chair, in particular, designed in 1952 for the Fritz Hansen furniture factory and made from a single piece of steam-bent plywood supported on a tubular steel frame, was his greatest contribution to the language of Modern furniture. Original, fresh, even sexy, it came to sum up the 1950s. Still much copied and now reproduced in a rainbow of colors, it continues to be one of the world's seminal Modern chairs.

Hard-line functionalism was being tamed and tempered throughout the world in the two decades after World War II. In Mexico, the great architect **Luis Barragán** also began exploring a more traditional, vernacular approach to building, introducing the use of brilliant color and local materials to the forms he had learned from Le Corbusier (pp. 108–9). In Italy, **Gio Ponti** helped to move Modernism into a lighter vein. Ponti, a true Renaissance man, who had been active as a teacher, writer, painter, architect, and product designer since the 1930s, was remarkable for his ability to integrate ceramics, furniture, and graphics with architecture.

ABOVE LEFT Bent-plywood chairs, by Alvar Aalto, at an exhibition of his work at the Museum of Modern Art, New York, 1938. A traveling version of the exhibition later toured U.S. architectural schools, including Yale and Harvard.

ABOVE RIGHT Arne Jacobsen in one of his Egg Chairs, designed in 1958. In the foreground is a mold for the chair.

OPPOSITE TOP The vibrantly colored Gilardi Residence, Mexico City, by Luis Barragán, 1975–77. The building was planned around the tree already established on the site.

OPPOSITE BELOW *Domus* magazine, 1948. Gio Ponti, its founding editor in 1928, was to use the magazine as a vehicle for his design philosophy on and off for fifty years.

In 1928, After studying architecture at Milan Polytechnic, Ponti had become founding editor of the influential *Domus* magazine, used initially as a mouthpiece for the Novecento group, founded by him in 1926. With its stripped-down classicism, the group might be regarded as an Italian form of Art Deco, but it was also profoundly influenced by the Austrian Wiener Werkstätte's belief that craft should be the basis of design. Ponti himself continued to design mainly for the craft-based industries.

From the 1930s Ponti worked with Cassina, one of Italy's most respected furniture manufacturers, and this relationship resumed after World War II, when he produced the enduring classic Superleggera Chair (1955), inspired by the light wooden chairs used by local fishermen. In the postwar years Ponti became one of Italy's most respected figures, partly through his renewed editorship of *Domus* and partly through his teaching at Milan Polytechnic, where he was to influence a generation of world-renowned product designers (pp. 110–11).

The essence of Italian design has been an ability to blend humor and excitement with a thorough but unstuffy respect for tradition. And for the hip generation of the 1950s two objects came to symbolize the new aesthetic of postwar Italian design: the Vespa scooter and the celebrated chrome espresso coffee machine designed by Ponti for La Pavoni in 1947. Forever associated with the new coffee bars, the latter, in particular, became part of a teenage lifestyle revealed in seminal novels of the period such as Colin McInnes's *Absolute Beginners.*

The Cabriolet Bed, by Joe Colombo, 1969. Colombo focused on creating space-saving products at affordable prices. This self-contained sleeping unit was originally designed for his own apartment and later mass produced. The headboard contains a radio, alarm clock, cigarette lighter, and ashtray, as well as storage. The tentlike electrically powered hood extends from the headboard for instant privacy.

The influence of Italy remained dominant throughout the 1960s, and Joe Colombo, a Milanese designer and architect who died at just forty, has become a legendary figure, arguably the most original and inventive of his generation. Incredibly versatile, he was an early adopter of such new materials as ABS plastic (a copolymer based on styrene), which allowed him to curve surfaces in three dimensions and gave him the freedom to invent extraordinary shapes. His objects became essays in abstract sculpture, and his furniture, with its interchangeable and moving parts, created an entirely new approach to interior design.

Indeed, in the 1960s new materials were again transforming furniture design in general, and the design movement of the next two decades altered people's preconceptions about furniture and interiors. The Danish designer Verner Panton was one of the most radical exponents, experimenting with boldly colored plastics, wire-framed seating, and surrealist lighting.

Panton and other experimental designers of the 1960s and 1970s worked with a wide range of industrially produced materials to take furniture that final step from handicraft to industrial design. The postwar developments in fiberglass, plastics, glass, Plexiglas, foam rubber, and synthetic textiles enabled them to instigate a revolution in the production of sophisticated mass-produced furniture. Panton himself was the first to succeed in designing a chair shaped and molded from a single piece of plastic, which finally eliminated the time-consuming hand labor and special finishing operations still required for mass-produced furniture.

But Panton was also important as a colorist. In keeping with the innovative, unpredictable shapes he designed, he made ample use of the new range of colors offered by modern industry, favoring strident reds, blues, yellows, and violet. In his use of lively colors, he moved away both from the colorlessness of functionalist design and from the naturalistic conventions of Scandinavian Modern (pp. 114–15).

Most significant of all, perhaps, was Panton's ability to subvert convention and introduce an element of surprise. And this was also to be the legacy of the idiosyncratic American architect John Lautner. A student of Frank Lloyd Wright's, Lautner was known for his bold geometry and exciting use of materials, as well as for his remarkable treatment of the relationship of landscape to structure (pp. 70–3, 84–9 and 116–117).

Much of Lautner's highly original and theatrical work also displayed extraordinary engineering skill. At Carling Residence (1947), for example, he devised a living room that pivoted on a turntable to become a patio, while at Chemosphere (1960), on its narrow 45-degree sloping site, he famously set a four-bedroom house shaped like a hexagonal flying saucer on top of a single hollow concrete column.

LEFT Chemosphere, Los Angeles, by John Lautner, 1960. Lautner was remarkable for his inventive and dramatic solutions to technical problems. Here in Hollywood, on a site too steep for conventional building, he created a wooden living platform sitting on top of a 30ft (9m) concrete stalk. The house is reached by funicular.

BELOW Verner Panton's most famous interior design project, the Phantasy Landscape, was the core of the 1970 Visiona 11 exhibition in Cologne, Germany. In radical room designs, Panton fused floor, wall, and ceiling treatments, and furniture, lighting, and textiles in extravaganzas of dramatic form and intense color.

The Smith Residence, Darien, Connecticut, by Richard Meier, 1965. Meier and his contemporaries—The Whites—believed that Le Corbusier had opened up a universe of pure form. Basing their work on the master's earliest principles, they developed a pure, white, formal architecture. Here, Meier creates a striking contrast between the pristine geometry of the house and the eternal beauty of the landscape.

By the 1970s, however, in the United States there was a return to a more purist approach to Modernism. In 1972 a group of architects known as The Whites (since practically all their buildings were white, inside and out) published a book called *Five Architects*, in which they expressed their desire to return to first principles, in particular to the early work of Le Corbusier.

Richard Meier, a leading member of the group, took up where Le Corbusier had left off, reworking his Cubist aesthetic with the benefit of the new materials of the late twentieth century. Many of the elements of Meier's design—vast, double-height windows, cylindrical structural columns, railings to ramps—derive from the classics of the early Modern Movement, in particular Le Corbusier's Villa Savoye (pp. 40–3 and 96) and Villa Stein. Yet Meier's architecture does develop an identity beyond that of his predecessor. Modern technology and new materials give Meier a flexibility undreamt of by Le Corbusier.

The early work of Le Corbusier continues to inspire. In Japan (which had been significantly affected by Western architecture since Frank Lloyd Wright arrived in Tokyo in 1916 to commence work on the Imperial Hotel), Le Corbusier's influence became widespread after World War II, when a whole generation of Japanese architects worked in his office and then returned to Japan to create an architecture of massive bold concrete forms.

In the 1980s Japanese architect **Tadao Ando** created a brilliant synthesis of western Modern Movement ideas and traditional Japanese sensibilities. Working from Le Corbusier's *Cinq Points*, he welded the simplicity and monumentalism of both forms to create havenlike interiors that offered a spiritual refuge from the pressure of contemporary life. His adherence to the smooth planes and easy access to outdoor spaces of Le Corbusier's aesthetic also, in many ways, brought architecture full circle, from Japan, which had inspired Wright in his free planning and partitioned spaces, back to Japan.

So the tradition continues. Modernism today constantly finds talented interpreters to adapt and reinvent it in response to the ever-shifting needs of modern life.

The Kidosaki Residence, Tokyo, Japan, by Tadao Ando, 1982–86. One of Japan's greatest contemporary architects, Tadao Ando has said that International Modernism is too clumsy an instrument to adapt to the needs of individual cultures. Yet, influenced by Le Corbusier, his extraordinarily beautiful designs contrive to meld Japan's unique relationship with nature and the pure, linear concrete of western Modernism. Here, in one of his small, courtyard houses, he furnishes the inhabitants with their own window on the natural world, a timeless bulwark against the chaotic speed of modern urban life.

CLASSIC Modern

The Fairchild Residence, Manhattan, New York, by George Nelson and William Hamby, 1941

A gallery overlooks the double-height living space.

Japanese references are evident in the doors to the garden terrace.

Frank Lloyd Wright
LA MINIATURA
PASADENA, CALIFORNIA, 1922–23

La Miniatura was the first in a series of four houses that Wright built in Los Angeles during the 1920s and that he named his textile-block houses. Designed for Alice Millard and sited in a narrow ravine in Pasadena, La Miniatura was one of Wright's solutions to the problem of providing affordable housing for the American middle classes.

In his search for an answer he looked anew at the precast concrete block, a factory product with little aesthetic appeal. "We would take that despised outcast of the building industry—the concrete block . . . find hitherto unsuspected soul in it—make it live as a thing of beauty—textured like the trees. All we would have to do would be to educate the concrete block, refine it, and knit it together with steel in the joints. The walls would thus become thin but solid reinforced slabs and yield to any desire for form imaginable."

Reinforced concrete had been used in beam form for cheap factory construction since the late 1880s, and Wright had used geometrically patterned blocks as early as 1913, in his Midway Gardens leisure complex in Chicago. His masterstroke here was to adapt both technologies to create a new type of building unit. Special molds were used to impose a shallow relief pattern (pierced and unpierced) on the faces of the blocks, which were then slotted together using reinforced steel set vertically and horizontally into preformed grooves. It was the arrangement of reinforcing steel that inspired Wright's description "textile block," and the unique character of these houses derives from the play of light and shade through the openings in the interlocked masses of concrete. As Wright himself put it, "The building now became a creation of interior space in light." On a more prosaic note, pierced blocks were glazed wherever they opened onto internal spaces—windows that must have been very difficult to clean.

Despite its intricate surface ornamentation, both externally and internally, La Miniatura is the closest Wright ever came to "a box on stilts"—his dismissive term for the white geometry of his European Modernist contemporaries. Abandoning the horizontal planes of his Prairie houses (pp. 14–15), he built vertically with no overhanging eaves: a simple parapet extends upward to create the surrounding wall of a roof terrace. Modest in scale and compact in design, the house is entered at the middle level, with the dining room and kitchen below and the double-height living space opening to a balcony in the front. The master bedroom is reached from a gallery at the rear of the living room.

In 1922 Frank Lloyd Wright had just returned from Japan, and the interior of La Miniatura has an oriental feel, something he continued to seek through much of his subsequent work. Externally, the densely ornamented blocks are more reminiscent of Mexico.

OPPOSITE Pierced blocks above the entrance to the garden terrace. Arches to the left join the house to the garages and create an opening to the garden.

The stairs from the lobby lead to the second floor.

Le Corbusier
VILLA SAVOYE
POISSY-SUR-SEINE, FRANCE, 1931

"The inhabitants come here because this rustic landscape goes well with country life. They survey their whole domain from the height of their jardin suspendu or from the four aspects of their fenêtres en longueur. Their domestic life is inserted in a Virgilian dream."

LE CORBUSIER

The Villa Savoye at Poissy-sur-Seine is one of the great defining buildings of the Modern Movement. Intended as "an architecture for everywhere" and proclaimed as such in Le Corbusier's *Oeuvre Complète*, its language—crisp, white geometrical shapes, strip windows, ramp—has been copied throughout the world. Light, ethereal, even magical, it has always defied categorization, critics likening it variously to a Palladian villa, a Classical temple, or a spaceship.

This was the last of a series of villas that Le Corbusier began building on the outskirts of Paris in the late 1920s, all of them used to explore and develop ideas first formalized in his *Cinq Points d'une Architecture Nouvelle* (see p. 21). But in the planning of the Villa Savoye, Le Corbusier had greater freedom than in any of the earlier projects. He was in the fortunate position that M. and Mme. Pierre Savoye were "quite without preconceived ideas, whether ancient or modern"; and the site—unlike the awkward, narrow plots of its predecessors—was an open space with greenery on all sides, offering him the opportunity to treat his building as an abstract sculpture to be seen in the round.

Le Corbusier's commitment to the automobile and the machine aesthetic is at once apparent. The house is designed so that the family could arrive by car from their Paris apartment, drive between the slender *pilotis* that support the main living area, and park beneath it in a garage that allowed for three vehicles. Indeed, the turning circle of the car determined the U-shape of the first-floor plan. Visitors enter the house through a recessed, glass-walled entrance lobby. Access to the second floor and the roof above is by stair or by a central ramp that rises up through the house. The remaining space at first-floor level is devoted to service areas.

At second-floor level a continuous long window punctuates and emphasizes the free façade, apparently sweeping around all four sides of the cube with little interruption and no variation. If you look more closely it becomes clear that in some places the horizontal strip is simply an opening onto a terrace. The almost square plan is complex and free-flowing. Rooms open into rooms, and half the area is devoted to the living room and a large garden terrace that is partially covered at one end. Large windows and sliding glass partitions between the terrace and the living room and hallway bring more daylight into the center of the house and create a flexible space for informal living (see also p. 96). Walls in the living room are washed in duck-egg blue or coral pink to enhance the changing natural light. On the third floor a curvilinear form marks out a small terrace for sunbathing.

The Savoye family furniture was not as severely Machine Age as that of the Stein family in their villa at Garches. Here, for example, there were no tubular-steel chairs, but Le Corbusier's inclusion of aluminum cabinet doors under all the long windows supplied an appropriately streamlined effect.

Unfortunately, his insistence on a machine aesthetic did not extend to an insistence on mechanical perfection, and clients and architect eventually fell out over such deficiencies as inadequate land drainage, water penetration through the skylights and ramp windows, and poor central heating.

ABOVE Load-bearing *pilotis* support the extended façade.

BELOW Seen from the adjoining bathroom, aluminum cabinets file under the long windows.

The living room opens onto the terrace.

Walter Gropius
THE GROPIUS RESIDENCE
LINCOLN, MASSACHUSETTS, 1937

Lincoln, Massachusetts, is a small country town within easy reach of Harvard. And it was here that Walter Gropius, then newly arrived from Britain to become Professor of Architecture at one of America's oldest universities, built three houses: one for himself and his wife, one for fellow architect Marcel Breuer, and one for the architectural historian James Ford.

Though stylistically the Gropius Residence derives in large part from the Cubist forms of Gropius's pre–World War II work in Dessau, here the founding director of the Bauhaus has turned a simple box into a dramatic sculptural statement. Externally, the severe geometry of the house is broken by the angled canopy of the traditional porch, which defines the entrance, and by the staccato fall of the black metal spiral staircase leading down from the roof terrace; the interior space is dramatized by a semicircular staircase. Significantly, the white-painted house uses the traditional wood-frame techniques of the area, but with the clapboard cladding laid vertically rather than horizontally.

Gropius was forced to take the vagaries of the New England climate into account in his siting of the house, positioning it on top of a gentle slope to take advantage of cooling breezes during the intense summer heat, and keeping the garage away from the house and near the road to make snow clearance easier. The northern face has a narrow strip of windows at second-floor level, while on the south, large windows open to two paved terraces, the larger of which juts far out into the garden and is covered with a flat roof. Gropius liked to play table tennis here. Also used as an outdoor eating area, it can be fully enclosed by screens.

The four-bedroom, four-bathroom house (also boasting a sewing room and a study) is economically planned. There are few corridors, and Gropius created a

The entrance punctuates the north façade.

tremendous sense of interlinking space, using minor rooms, such as the study and second-floor dressing-rooms, as transitional interludes between the main staircase and the primary living rooms and bedrooms.

Though purist in its simplicity, internally the house has none of the austerity of Gropius's work during the Weimar period. True, it was furnished with the simple steel-framed, bent-plywood pieces so characteristic of Marcel Breuer and decorated with vibrant paintings by Lázló Moholy-Nagy and Xanti Schawinsky, but it is warmed by a cork-tile floor which contributes to an atmosphere of relaxed comfort that is more North American than North European.

The house remains the perfect evocation of that period in American architecture when the masters of the European Modern Movement hit the East Coast with such dynamism: a clean-lined expression of the International Style in a clapboard guise.

Wood and steel define the curve of the stair.

The view of the house from the west; to the far right is the larger, covered terrace

Patrick Gwynne + Wells Coates

THE HOMEWOOD
ESHER, SURREY, ENGLAND, 1938

One of three window bays in the living room

Patrick Gwynne was just twenty-four when he persuaded his parents to let him design their new house. Comdr. and Mrs. Gwynne had lived on the 10-acre (4-hectare) property for nearly twenty-five years in a house that, by 1938, was desperately in need of repair and modernization and close to an increasingly busy main road. Patrick had been working for the architect-engineer Wells Coates (p. 24), and Coates helped with the design and put Gwynne in touch with reliable contractors familiar with the new technology.

Gwynne and Coates demolished the existing Victorian building and sited the new house in woodland farther from the road. A two-story structure, the new house has two wings that are set at right angles and linked by a small staircase block. All the living space is on the raised second floor, with one wing containing the bedrooms and bathrooms; the other, larger, L-shaped main wing, the living and dining rooms, kitchen and pantry areas, and servants' quarters. The first floor is devoted to the entrance, the garages, other services, servant accommodation, an isolated study, and, beneath the living room, a wide covered terrace open to the garden. The house was sited to gain all-day sun and the best views and privacy for the reception rooms.

Gwynne had traveled on the Continent, visiting such landmarks of Modernism as the Weissenhof estate (p. 21); and the influence of Le Corbusier's 1920s villas floating on their slender *pilotis* (p. 41) is evident. The Homewood is raised on column supports, standing free where the terrace runs under the main wing and where the drive runs under the bedroom wing. The first-floor brick wall is set back to display its non-load-bearing nature. The continuous band of windows running the length of the east façade is also pure Corbusier.

With the garden already beautifully landscaped by Gwynne's father, Gwynne and Coates were determined to emphasize the relationship of house to nature, and the link between indoors and out, so fundamental to the Modernist aesthetic, contributes equally to the success of this design. The house is poised over the garden, closely linked but detached and always dominating as the garden flows beneath it. There are two entrances uniting house with garden; one in the staircase block, where great windows at both levels allow visitors wonderful views across the garden from the sweeping cantilevered stairway, the other in the balcony beyond the second-floor dining room, from which a wide concrete staircase juts dramatically into the garden.

The interior is lavish—a virtuoso display of the latest technology, the finest materials, and the most fashionable furniture and fixtures. The doors are leather covered, the walls faced with marble and walnut, the floors lined with maple. Most of the furniture was designed by Gywnne (who still lives in the house). In the informal main living space, he has arranged seating near the windows for daylight hours, near the fire for evenings. For parties the room can be made even larger by opening the folding doors to the dining room and the closed balcony beyond.

The view of the bedroom wing with first-floor study from the staircase block.

The bedroom wing viewed from the drive; to the right is part of the L-shaped main wing.

The other two window bays of the living room—beyond the dining room and the balcony.

George Nelson + William Hamby

THE FAIRCHILD RESIDENCE
NEW YORK, 1941

George Nelson had studied in Rome in the early 1930s and, while there, interviewed leading figures in the Modern Movement. He returned to the United States full of the belief that "everything that is worth anything is always modern because it can't be anything else, and therefore there are no flags to wave, no manifestoes. You just do the only thing you can honestly do *now*." With an attitude such as this, it is hardly surprising that he refused to subscribe to the critique of the International Style as outlined by Hitchcock and Johnson (see p. 26). He believed in applying fresh ideas and fresh solutions to each new problem. "For the modern architect who knows his trade, planning and design, building and site, houses and family, all form a single package. The product he creates is a live thing. It fits the people for whom it was designed, it expresses the time they live in, and, above all, it works psychologically as well as physically. It does all these things because it was conceived in a creative manner and not taken out of a copybook."

One of the least copybook and most significant buildings Nelson was to design in his relatively brief career as an architect was the Fairchild Residence, a lavish town house built for the aircraft manufacturer Sherman Fairchild on New York's Upper East Side. A bachelor who entertained a great deal and frequently worked from home, Fairchild wanted a house with generous reception and office space, as well as a self-contained apartment for a member of his family. It took eighteen months to plan and eighteen months to build, with Fairchild himself closely involved in its evolution.

The house broke radically with tradition, particularly in its plan. The typical New York town house had views of the street at the front and views of fire escapes behind, with the dark center of the house taken up by the stairwell, services, and bathrooms. Nelson and his partner, William Hamby, decided to split the 100- x 25-foot (30.5 x 7.6m) site into two and position the majority of the rooms facing onto a central, glass-walled atrium containing a tree-filled courtyard (see *Fortune* cover, p. 27). This gave the house two south-facing aspects and introduced much greater natural light throughout. At the back of the house, beyond the central atrium, were the first-floor living room and a study above. At the front, in the four-story elevation, were the maids' rooms, kitchen, dining room, separate second-floor apartment and third-floor master bedroom suite. Ramps, rather than staircases, linked the levels.

Internally the house was quite literally an up-to-date "machine for living," with electrically operated venetian blinds on the outside of the windows, air conditioning, soundproofing, and a resilient teak floor mounted on rubber springs. The lighting and much of the furnishing, already one of Nelson's preoccupations, were of the latest design.

On the right, the façade: the site was later redeveloped.

Louvres shade the study window.

"Preconceived ideas are poison. It is a pretty safe rule that if a planning solution is thoroughly workable it is not going to be difficult to design an exterior which will be agreeable in appearance. It may be unconventional. Maybe the bathrooms will have big windows instead of little ones. Maybe the kitchen will be next to the front door instead of the back door. Maybe it won't even look like a house at all to those who are accustomed to symmetrical fronts with two shutters on every window. Nevertheless, in its personal, modern way, it will be a good-looking house."

GEORGE NELSON AND HENRY WRIGHT

OPPOSITE Courtyard and ramps (right), looking towards the living room.
RIGHT Small ceiling spots above the table supply the direct light.

A narrow ramp leads to the main entrance.

Harry Seidler

THE ROSE SEIDLER RESIDENCE
WAHROONGA, N.S.W., AUSTRALIA, 1950

Harry Seidler had just finished working for Marcel Breuer in New York when he arrived in Australia on a visit to his parents in the late 1940s. Still very much under the influence of his Harvard tutors Walter Gropius and Breuer (pp. 19 and 28), his first project was to look for a tract of land on which he could build a community of houses to accommodate his family and friends. Eventually one was found—a generous site of sloping bushland just north of Sydney with panoramic views of the Kuring-gai Chase National Park. Three houses were ultimately erected on the 16-acre (6.5-hectare) site—Rose Seidler Residence, Rose Residence, and Seidler Residence—but the first and the most significant was that built for his parents, the Rose Seidler Residence.

The house is instantly recognizable as a product of the Modern Movement: a clean, white, translucent box above a basement garage, open on all sides, raised above the ground on *pilotis* and anchored to it by a ramp. In plan it is a spacious, free-flowing square with a central open terrace and a two-story light well illuminating the core of the building. Living and sleeping areas are linked by a family room.

Just as important as the structure and plan are the decoration and furnishing. Seidler used an essentially monochromatic palette —light gray walls, medium-gray carpets, and rooms subdivided by black wall cabinets, desks, and kitchen benches. This is accented with strong color—blues, yellows, and red—which echo the colors in the exterior mural painted by Seidler himself, which runs the length of the terrace and follows the depth of the light well to ground level. The furniture and lighting were all imported from New York and represented the best of contemporary design. The dining and lounge chairs are by Charles Eames, the Knoll Grasshopper chair by and Eero Saarinen, the cutlery by Russel Wright.

Australia had remained largely untouched by the theory and practice of the Modernists, and the house had instant impact. Economically planned and built, it was immediately recognized as an attractive and affordable option for the expanding Australian middle class. Harry Seidler went on to become one of Australia's leading architects, but in this uncompromising first creation, with its transparent, geometric composition, raised elevation, ramp, and homage to art, he laid down the hallmarks of his style.

Natural stone cladding adds texture to the concrete structure.

High-gloss color spikes the monochrome.

"There can be no more captive client than a mother. . . . [She] agreed to sell all her Viennese furniture, but refused to part with her elaborately decorated silver cutlery. Whenever I came to dinner, only the Russel Wright stainless-steel flatware I brought from New York was allowed to be seen."

HARRY SEIDLER

High-gloss color spikes the monochrome.

The role of concrete is clearly expressed across the façade.

Le Corbusier
MAISONS JAOUL
NEUILLY-SUR-SEINE, FRANCE, 1951–55

From as early as the 1930s Le Corbusier began to move away from the principles he had outlined in his *Cinq Points d'une Architecture Nouvelle* (p. 21). His work lost much of its attachment to the Purist geometry and machine aesthetic of the villas of the 1920s and became more individualistic and tactile, more responsive to site and location, and more vernacular in feel. The pair of relatively modest houses he built for André Jaoul, head of foreign relations at the Société d'Electro-Chimie d'Ugine, and his family of four sons, in the leafy Paris suburb of Neuilly, was to become one of the most influential examples of this new style.

The site itself was problematic—narrow and sloping with a high wall from a neighboring property lining one side. Le Corbusier tackled its limitations by designing two long, thin houses set at right angles to one another on a terrace constructed in part of foundation spoils. A central courtyard links the buildings, which otherwise enjoy relative privacy. Both houses are built to a similar plan, with the entrance hall, kitchen, and open-plan living space on the first floor, three or four bedrooms on the second, and one or two bedrooms on the third. One of the houses also has a small chapel on the second floor.

Here the principles of the *Cinq Points* have been overturned. The curved roofs—no longer flat terraces—are planted with grass. The *fenêtres en longueur* have been abandoned in preference for rectangular and square framed windows, arranged within paneled wooden inserts. And the garage—so crucial to the imagery of "the machine for living in"—lies underground, beneath the terrace.

The most radical shift, however, was Le Corbusier's approach to materials and building methods. *Pilotis* are abandoned, and the Jaoul houses are constructed of solid brick walls with concrete ceilings and floors. The frame was assembled by workmen using hammers and nails, while the parallel vaulted ceilings of the interior were formed by pouring light concrete over arches constructed of Catalan brick tiles.

Stylistically the houses owe much to the vernacular of the Mediterranean, in particular to the farmhouses of Provence. The deliberate crudeness of the brickwork, the bold exposure of the plywood facings, the rough surfaces of the shuttered concrete, both inside and out, still have the power to shock—particularly in contrast to the hard, textureless finish and Classical geometry of the houses that preceded them.

These expressive surfaces, however, and the vigorous use of contrasting materials, have had as enduring an impact as the rationalist ideals of the early Modern Movement.

Wall color brings even greater warmth to the interior.

The principal vault runs the length of the kitchen.

The first-floor staircase block leads down into the kitchen.

The main wing's sloping roof accommodates a second story at one end.

Viewed from the gallery, the living room is constructed from high-level glazed partitions.

Arne Jacobsen
THE RUTHWEN-JÜRGENSEN RESIDENCE
SKODSBORG, DENMARK, 1956

Although his native Denmark was relatively isolated, with a strong tradition of Neoclassicism, Jacobsen had seen the work of Ludwig Mies van der Rohe and Le Corbusier at the Paris exhibition of 1925 (p. 21). By the 1930s he was designing in a sophisticated mixture of Danish vernacular and Continental Modernism, and after World War II Frank Lloyd Wright and Mies van der Rohe were his major influences. This lavish villa on the outskirts of Copenhagen demonstrates a mastery of Wright's sensitivity to landscape and Mies's immaculate Classicism in a work of distinction and originality.

Jacobsen made the most of the house's privileged site, overlooking the Oresund, the sound between Denmark and Sweden, with an ingenious three-wing plan, setting the house on a platform that runs eastward beyond the house to form a high terrace above the shore. The principal wing, in the center, is placed to take advantage of the eastward view across the water and of the afternoon sun in the west. The southerly wing articulates outward, forming an obtuse angle that acts in part as a windbreak for the rest of the house. Services are sited below the platform in the central wing. The main entrance is through the west-facing courtyard at the rear.

The central wing is constructed of steel and clad with timber, inside and out. It is the lightness of the structure, with walls partitioning a series of luminous interiors, that gives the house its defining transparency. To counterpoint that effect and anchor the central section, the north-facing façades of the other two (single-story) wings are of painted brick with large wood-framed windows facing south.

Like many of his Scandinavian contemporaries, Jacobsen was also involved with the design of the interior. Here, in close collaboration with the owner, he designed most of the furniture, and supervised the landscaping and planting of the garden. Unmannered, without cliché or gimmick, the house remains a model of precision and elegance.

Glazed gallery walls heighten the sense of transparency.

The latest in labor-saving technology was part of the carefree vision.

Pierre Koenig

CASE STUDY HOUSE NO. 21
HOLLYWOOD HILLS, CALIFORNIA, 1958

"As outdoor living became more important, we felt that houses should reflect this. Outdoor space became a continuation of indoor space. . . . Glass was used to extend indoor space visually. Kitchens were turned around so that meals could be served directly from the kitchen to the outdoors."

PIERRE KOENIG

Pierre Koenig was a latecomer to John Entenza's Case Study House Program, but many consider his Case Study House No. 21—the Bailey Residence—its most significant contribution. Entenza asked the thirty-five-year-old to join his roster of architects in 1957, after a number of Koenig's earlier houses had appeared in *Arts & Architecture*. "Pierre," he said, "if you ever have a good house, with some good clients, tell me and we'll make it a Case Study House." Koenig's response: "All of my houses were with good clients, so I just said, 'I have one now.'" The "good clients" were psychologist Walter Bailey and his wife, Mary, who had commissioned Koenig to design a two-bedroom, two-bathroom, open-plan house on a level site in the Hollywood Hills.

Over the preceding five years Koenig had carried out extensive research into steel-framed housing, and in March 1957 *Arts & Architecture* published his designs for a low-cost house that could be factory built and assembled quickly on site. Paraphrasing Le Corbusier, Koenig described it as "a house made just like a car." At No. 21, he continued, in the spirit of the Program, to rely on ready-made products and prefabricated steel beams delivered to the site in one piece.

The relationship of house to nature—another Program fundamental—was crucial. Koenig opened up the interior in a variety of ways. He ran a moatlike pool around the house, supplying each of the main rooms with its own brick-paved terrace, and he created an internal courtyard, filled with plants, a small pool, and a fountain, accessed from the kitchen-dining area and from the living room.

Furnishing was significant too. For the streamlined kitchen he specified the latest General Electric combined sink, range, and dishwasher with a stainless-steel counter and wall-hung refrigerator. Vinyl flooring fulfilled the Baileys' desire for easy maintenance.

Case Study House No. 21 perfectly exemplified Entenza's ideal of affordable, mass-produced housing, and in 1959 *Arts & Architecture* hailed it as "a design that . . . represents some of the cleanest and most immaculate thinking in the development of the small contemporary house." An icon of the period, this elegant, austere pavilion captures the optimism of the 1950s and is seen by architects worldwide as a seminal single-family house.

ABOVE The steel-framed carport extends from the main body of the house.

BELOW When the house was presented to the public after completion, none of the clients' furniture was allowed to ruin the effect.

OPPOSITE AND BELOW Within the open-plan living space, deep-pile carpet defined "conversation areas."

A curving *brise-soleil* shades the entrance hall.

A skylight recalls the shape of the pool.

John Lautner
THE CONCANNON RESIDENCE
BEVERLY HILLS, CALIFORNIA, 1960

This single-story house on a steep, forested site in Beverly Hills is one of the lesser known designs of John Lautner. It is, nonetheless, a fine example of the work of a master of complex, nonrectilinear space. Like the drawings of the artist Paul Klee, Lautner's architecture "takes a line for a walk," creating along the way an extraordinary sense of dynamic space. His unique, dramatic buildings offer their inhabitants a liberation from the conventions of the traditional enclosure, providing, in the words of the house's current occupant, "Space to live and breathe and be creative. While being a great piece of architecture in itself, it is not intrusive. It leaves a lot open for you."

Cantilevered into the sloping hillside, the house appears to hover above its site. In plan and elevation it is a free-form working of overlapping arcs, operating over slight and subtle gradations of level, unanchored by a central core. The curve is its leitmotif, reiterated in the tentlike roof supported on thin pipelike mullions, in the curving walls, in the sinuous outline of the jutting façade, and even in the terrazzo flooring as it sweeps down to a high-angled curb near the steps to the entrance hall. Out-of-doors, the double convex of the eye-shaped pool repeats the theme, becoming symbolically the all-seeing focus of the house.

But the manipulation of light and the relationship of house to nature are as fundamental to Lautner's work as his intricate geometry and technical mastery. Here, daylight and sunlight are cunningly deployed through a variety of carefully considered apertures. The cagelike fenestration of the main living space, the skylight cut into the tentlike roof, the delicate tracery of the *brise-soleil* on the poolside wall, all play skillfully with light and shade in the brilliant California sunshine, rendering the boundaries of the house insubstantial as indoors and outdoors dissolve and unite.

In the mid-1990s the house was bought by Jim Goldstein, owner of the neighboring Sheats-Goldstein Residence, also by Lautner. Goldstein has always intended to demolish it and build a tennis court and a guest house to Lautner's design on the site. For the moment, therefore, its future is uncertain.

The dressing room–library opens onto a curved balcony overlooking a steep slope.

LEFT A curving line of closets extends across the dressing room–library wall.

OPPOSITE Shallow steps lead down to the main living space; kitchen, bedroom, and library are on the raised level

Richard Neutra
THE INADOMI RESIDENCE
SILVERLAKE, CALIFORNIA, 1960

The view from the family room–kitchen with own design chair.

Neutra's residential work of the 1950s and 1960s broke with the crisp, cool machine imagery of his prewar years. His later houses became much softer and more relaxed, as he moved from a reliance on aluminum, concrete, and stucco to a preference for natural materials and warmer colors. His client base, too, shifted during this period. In the 1920s and 1930s he had designed mainly for a small group of avant-garde enthusiasts, but by the 1950s and 1960s his clientele was more mainstream, as the middle class embraced Modernism enthusiasm.

The Inadomi Residence is typical of the work of this period—a relaxed, contemporary home intended for a middle-class couple and their four active children. Built as part of a community of Neutra-designed residences overlooking Silverlake, it is close to the architect's own home and atelier of almost forty years. It is one of a pair of dwellings that Neutra designed to form the fourth side of a square, completing a group of houses begun earlier.

His awareness of nature and his skill at siting and landscaping remain as strong as ever. The modest two-story dwelling digs well into its hillside site, sloping up by the equivalent of one floor to the southeast, and a grove of trees partially screens the lake frontage. The house is oriented in two directions, with the living room and all the bedrooms facing the lake, while the kitchen-dining-study area opens to the pool and the hills behind. Living and dining rooms are placed on the upper level to make best use of the views, and the entrance is midway between the two floors to give maximum privacy.

Neutra's later houses are far more spatially complex than his earlier work, and the subtle interplay of volume and intersecting axes, together with a far greater use of plate glass, is apparent here. The plan is open and airy throughout. At the entrance, thin piano wires serve as the only balustrade for the short flights of steps that leads down to the bedrooms and up to the expansive main living spaces. There, a central fireplace and a half-height folding wooden screen are the only separation between the living room and family room–kitchen.

The move to a friendlier, warmer, more textured design is clear. The fireplace, for instance, is a masterly counterpoint of three earthy materials: the great extended hearth, of common brick; the box and surrounding areas, of narrow Roman brick; and the wall above, of vertical bands of rough blond stone. The floor in the family room–kitchen is cork. And the color spectrum has shifted, too. In place of the sophisticated white grays of the Lovell Health House (p. 17), here we have the upbeat tones of modern California.

Texture is explored and exploited in the family room–kitchen.

Earth tones color the screen in the dining area.

Light floods through the house.

Hanne Kjærholm
THE KJÆRHOLM RESIDENCE
RUNGSTED, DENMARK, 1961

In 1961 Hanne Kjærholm, a Danish architect of international standing who still teaches at Copenhagen's Royal Academy of Art, designed a four-bedroom home for her family in Rungsted, just north of Copenhagen. A fine piece of Danish Modernism in itself, the house was also—and remains—a private showcase for the furniture of Hanne's husband, Poul Kjærholm, who died in 1980. It is still laid out as he intended.

The single-story structure is perched on the edge of a plateau bordering the Oresund, the stretch of water separating Denmark and Sweden. Pressed close upon the shoreline, it is unprotected by garden or terrace, with the long rectangular living-dining-working room fronting the water through an uninterrupted series of plate-glass windows. Along this façade runs a portico of whitewashed pillars. "I put in a portico," explains Hanne Kjærholm, "because the horizon is so large it could easily have become overwhelming. [It] acts like an arch on a stage, making the distance more manageable."

In plan, too, the house displays a Classical geometry. Almost square, it is constructed around three rows of twelve square columns with the open-plan living space occupying the front half of the square and running the entire width of the frontage. The middle row of columns divides the living area from the sleeping area at the rear. Three bedrooms are now symmetrically planned around the kitchen, heating, and two bathrooms. "In the old-fashioned way," says Kjærholm, "the fireplace is the center of the house"—though the house was, in fact, one of the first in Denmark to employ underfloor heating.

As with much Scandinavian design at this period, the use of materials is central to the creation of a warm, protective interior, a bulwark against the sometimes ferocious conditions outside. Here, the walls of whitewashed brick and pine paneling, the woven sisal covering the floor, and the widespread use of wood and leather supply a cozy intimacy. "It was an inexpensive house to build, but I do very much care about the details and the materials, and though I have not changed anything it has lasted very well. It was very well built," says Hanne Kjærholm, who still lives in the house.

The furnishing, of course, is dominated by the work of Poul Kjærholm, who for many years was Professor of Furniture Design at the Royal Academy of Fine Arts in Copenhagen, and who is now acknowledged to be one of the greats of the golden age of Danish Modernism in the 1950s and 1960s. In the late '50s Kjærholm broke with the Danish tradition of handcrafted furniture, substituting tubular steel and chrome—materials favored by the Modernists—for the more traditional wood.

Often cantilevered, with seats of luxurious leather, woven cane, or canvas, Poul Kjærholm's work is distinguished by its refinement and by the impeccable detailing that gives it an almost handmade appearance. And whereas much Bauhaus furniture still looks severe in the home, Kjærholm's seductive and now hugely popular pieces successfully bridge the gap between the public arena and the less formal demands of the private space.

The pillared portico punctuates the façade and manages the view.

"Though it's forty years old, the house is still modern, and my husband's furniture seems more modern now than when he was alive."

HANNE KJÆRHOLM

Wooden blinds filter the northern light.

OPPOSITE The formal entrance hall.

Natural materials and textures in the Scandinavian tradition warm the interior.

The front entrance.

The double-height living space.

John Lautner
THE WALSTROM RESIDENCE
BEVERLY HILLS, CALIFORNIA, 1969

Douglas Walstrom, a retired electrical engineer from the aerospace industry, first became interested in the work of John Lautner after reading an article on him in *The Los Angeles Times*. Invited to design a house on a steep and difficult site in Beverly Hills, Lautner approached the project with his usual inventiveness and technical mastery, offering Walstrom and his wife, Olivia, three solutions—a tower, three concrete cylinders, or an irregular wooden cube. The last option was eventually chosen and built.

The 1,400 square-foot (130m²) cabinlike dwelling was constructed on two levels, with two bedrooms on the lower level and the main living space and a third bedroom above. Except for its foundation walls and some diagonal beams, the house floats free of the ground, propped off the slope to look back at the narrow entry path that zigzags down to the carport far below. The plan is trapezoid, a four-sided form with two parallel sides of unequal length. Although more rectilinear than much of Lautner's work, the house still demonstrates the sculptural qualities that distinguish all his designs.

The simple roof slopes dramatically above the main, freely composed living space, which at its highest point is illuminated by banks of double-height windows. In one corner a great wedge-shaped gallery bisects the space horizontally. It is supported by a tall bookcase block that also conceals the bathroom. Reached by a suspended staircase, the gallery is the third bedroom, the TV room, and a place for the grandchildren to play. Above, in the sloping roof, wooden rafters radiate from the shorter to the longer parallel wall. A conventional eye might have relied upon a sunburst effect. By contrast, Lautner gradually increases the distance between the beams from one side of the room to the other. By subverting the expected, he injects a sense of movement and drama into the space.

Here his leitmotif is a particular wedge shape. Referred to again and again—in the zigzag path from the carport, the gallery bulkhead, the pitch of the roof, and the great wall beams of the main living space—it serves to unify his complex spatial geometry.

Cedar was used throughout the building, and you can still smell the sap. As always with Lautner, that relationship with nature is fundamental. The house, with windows on all sides, is like the mountain retreat of some primitive tribe, hugged by the surrounding trees and grassy hillside. Indeed, the hillside garden flows under the very center of the house itself. The winding path that draws visitors toward the building becomes an internal ramp, passing around the house from flank to flank and glazed on one side to reveal the ferns and shrubs of the "underground" garden. On the lower floor, too, glazed walls in the master bedroom and the guest bedroom open up the opposite view. Once through the house, the path continues to the top of the hill, now as a series of timber "stepping-stones." There, a leveled area shaded by mature trees offers space for reflection.

Below the gallery bedroom, book stacks conceal the corner bathroom.

"The thing is to be able to hold, and try to pull together, all the possible emotional elements, physical elements, structural elements, and nature, and try to pull that into an idea. One idea."

JOHN LAUTNER

The recurring wedge shape can be seen in the stair as it slices space and in the glazed wall sections beyond.

At one side of the living space the roof slopes low over the kitchen-dining area.

The stairs from the gallery bedroom lead down to the main living space.

The gallery houses a built-in bed platform.

The ramp between front and back doors and a view of the "underground" garden.

Modern **TRADEMARKS**

La Miniatura, Los Angeles, California, by Frank Lloyd Wright, 1922–23

FRANK LLOYD WRIGHT

plan and features PRAIRIE HOUSES: rambling and horizontal, terraces, low roofs with wide overhangs, bands of windows / LATER: more open areas, closer relationship with natural world

materials stone / many different types of brick / metal cladding / widespread use of wood / PRAIRIE HOUSES: stained glass / TEXTILE-BLOCK HOUSES: ornamented prefabricated concrete / LATER: large expanses of unleaded glass

color muted / brighter hues to highlight

furniture wooden / built-in or custom-built for specific projects

lighting designed for individual projects

TOP Fallingwater, Bear Run, Pennsylvania, 1935–37. Wright's bands of painted concrete combine with natural stone to reflect the forms in the rocks below—a perfect blend of building and landscape.

ABOVE LEFT Storer Residence, Los Angeles, 1923: an earlier use of concrete. A view of the double-height living room from the terrace demonstrates the richly patterned concrete surfaces typical of Wright's textile-block houses of the early 1920s (see also pp. 38–39).

ABOVE RIGHT Robie Residence, Chicago, Illinois, 1908–09. Much of Wright's work contained furniture designed specifically for it. Strongly rectilinear, crafted in traditional materials (such as wood and stone, with metal detailing) and frequently built-in, it perfectly complemented his architecture. The arms of the simple wooden sofa, made specially for this Prairie house, are extended to create a table on either side.

MIES VAN DER ROHE

plan and features rectilinear, divided by flat planes or service blocks / widespread use of glass to bring outside in / flat roofs

materials fixed plate glass / marble floors and walls / steel pillars and columns / wood-paneled walls

color natural

furniture own designs / grouped to define areas / built-in

TOP German Pavilion, Barcelona, Spain, 1929 (p. 22). It was here that Mies first demonstrated many of the characteristics of his style to public acclaim. The marble-faced walls sandwiched between floor and ceiling slabs, the extravagant range of expensive materials (travertine and onyx), the chrome-plated steel, and green and transparent glass, plus the immaculate detailing, were to define his work.

ABOVE The Barcelona Chair, 1929. Designed specifically for the German Pavilion, Barcelona, the chair, like the building itself, is stately and elegant, setting two rectangular leather cushions, supported by leather straps, on an X-shaped steel frame. The quality of its materials and its lightness and simplicity have made it, for many people, symbolic of the very essence of Modernism. It has been in continuous production since 1948.

LE CORBUSIER

plan and features free-flowing main living spaces / structured bedroom areas / internal courtyards and roof terraces with direct access to interior / large expanses of glass

materials EARLY WORK: concrete, rendered brick, aluminum / LATER: raw brick, shuttered concrete, wood

color EARLY WORK: predominantly white exteriors, with pastel hues to lighten interiors / LATER: **brighter hues to highlight textures**

furniture bentwood armchair by Thonet / chromed or enamelled tubular-steel seating with leather upholstery / animal-hide rugs / built-in

lighting daylight essential / occasional / uplight

TOP A view from the living room into the internal courtyard of the Villa Savoye, 1931. The whitewashed concrete walls, the ramp, the *fenêtres en longueur*, the lateral fenestration on the ramp windows, the plate-glass window, and the quarry-tiled floor are all characteristic of this first phase of Le Corbusier's work (pp. 40–43). The tubular-steel and leather Chaise Longue (1929), designed in collaboration with Charlotte Perriand, demonstrates Le Corbusier's belief that furniture should be incorporated in the design of a house (p. 21).

ABOVE A concrete and glazed screen at the Unité d'Habitation, Marseilles, 1952 (p. 21). The "brutalist", textural finish of the concrete in this dramatic, municipally financed apartment block in the south of France was adopted worldwide.

MARCEL BREUER

plan and features square and rectangular rooms, leading into each other / changes of level / large sliding glass doors and windows / terraces / mainly flat roofs or roofs sloping from one side

materials EARLIER DESIGNS: painted, rendered brick or concrete / LATER: painted brick and natural stone with wooden inserts / timber-clad ceilings / stone or tiled floors

color mostly natural / external and internal brick, painted white or in primary hues

furniture built-in / wallmounted / EARLY WORK: bent aluminum and tubular chrome / LATER: bent-plywood

TOP Neumann Residence, Croton-on-Hudson, New York, 1953. The natural stone floor and painted brick fireplace, the use of wood, and the interplay of textures and light, are typical of Breuer's architectural design, as is the painted brick wall of the exterior.

ABOVE The Long Chair, designed for the British company Isokon in 1935 and still in production, demonstrates Breuer's revolutionary use of bent plywood. Breuer had recognized the potential of the material while head of carpentry at the Bauhaus and used it in some of his first tubularsteel furniture. The form, too, recalls a chair he originally made in slatted aluminum. On his arrival in Britain in 1935 he was commissioned by the founder of Isokon, Jack Pritchard, to design an entire range of plywood furniture, and in addition to the Long Chair, Breuer produced designs for stacking chairs, sofas, armchairs, and nesting tables (p. 18). With its comfortable curved seat and back and stretched fabric upholstery, the Long Chair remained influential for years.

ALVAR AALTO

plan and features free-flowing, open-plan spaces on different levels / irregular, asymmetric, and organic forms / large fireplaces

materials whitewashed brick / timber-clad curved ceilings / rattan-wrapped pillars / wooden screens / fabric-covered walls / quarry-tiled floors / printed fabrics and woven animal-based designs, such as zebra stripes

color white and natural hues used with black

furniture molded and bent-plywood / upholstered sofas / natural fibers and textures / built-in storage

lighting own designs / freestanding / pendant

TOP Villa Mairea, Turku, Finland, 1938. The wooden ceiling is typical of Aalto's work, both domestic and public, and creates a warm contrast to the polished quarry tiles on the floor. The freestanding pillars act both as sculptural definition of the space and as an exposed structural element. The furniture is placed in groups to delineate the distinct functions of the open-plan room. The corner fireplace is another Aalto trademark.

ABOVE LEFT A first-floor view of the double-height pole screens that define the stair at the Villa Mairea. A pierced plywood balustrade reasserts the horizontal perspective at the upper level.

ABOVE RIGHT Aalto's sketch for the Savoy Vase, 1936. Created for a fashionable restaurant in Finland, for which Aalto had also designed the interior, the characteristically fluid, organic shape broke with the tradition of symmetrical, geometric glass produced by most of his contemporaries.

CHARLES & RAY EAMES

plan and features rectilinear, with room flowing into room / double-height spaces with galleries

materials standard, prefabricated frames / steel-framed windows / plywood stairtreads / ceramic tiling / fiberglass screens / parquet floors / wooden wall finishes

color primaries

furniture own designs / plywood / fiberglass / leather / steel-rod / aluminum / vinyl / built-in storage

lighting recessed / occasional / wallmounted / freestanding

TOP Eames Residence, Case Study House No. 8, 1949 (p. 29). The Eameses mixed their collection of ethnic belongings with own-design furniture, setting both casually within the elegant, airy, double-height interior. All the built-in furniture in the house derives from, or became, mass-produced lines by Eames. The seating inspired the later Sofa Compact, and the shelving and plywood storage with sliding doors of different materials became the ESU range.

ABOVE LEFT The exterior of the Eames Residence. The steel ready-made frame is inset with glass panels in a Mondrian-inspired grid and color scheme.

ABOVE RIGHT The Eames Lounge Chair and Ottoman (1955–56) is one of the twentieth century's most popular furniture designs. The chair is made of three separate leather cushions, each with a molded plywood back, mounted on a swiveling aluminum base. It was the first mass-production chair to rival the comfort of the traditional upholstered armchair.

RICHARD NEUTRA

plan and features usually single story / open plan, with areas screened or divided for different functions / integration of indoors and out, with most rooms opening onto terraces or courtyards / sliding glass windows and doors / flat roofs or roofs sloping from one side / water features

materials metal or wood frames / aluminum or wood cladding / wood-paneled walls / concrete, brick, or cork flooring / cut-stone fireplaces

color muted neutrals / brighter hues for contrast on built-in seating

furniture built-in, veneered, or painted / own-design steel-framed chairs and tables / low room dividers

lighting recessed downlighters / concealed in dropped ceilings / freestanding

TOP Singleton Residence, Los Angeles, 1959. With its steel frame, its use of natural stone, its deployment of surrounding water, and its integration of house and landscape, this house encapsulates Neutra's California style.

ABOVE LEFT Two typical space dividers—the vertically cut stone fireplace and the folding screen at the Inadomi Residence, 1960.

ABOVE RIGHT A corner window overlooking the lake below the Inadomi Residence (pp. 74–77). Neutra highlighted the elegant neutrality of his color schemes with contrasting hues, applied most frequently to built-in seating.

PIERRE KOENIG

plan and features rectilinear, sometimes L-shaped / kitchen islands or galleys / sliding glass doors / central patios and courtyards / pools and carports

materials steel frames / concrete and vinyl-tiled flooring / brick pavers for terracing / masonite partitioning for walls / mosaic in service areas

color monochrome / accent hues on small accessories, such as throw pillows

furniture own designs / contemporary pieces (such as Eames and Mies van der Rohe) / formal groups in center of room

lighting daylight in center of house from courtyards / track / recessed

TOP For Koenig, industry was architecture's future, and in his Case Study House No. 22 (1959), with its steel-frame construction, open-plan living space, vast areas of plate glass, and California lifestyle pool, the future had definitely arrived. The kitchen, with its ceiling-mounted cabinets and state-of-the-art modern appliances, remains a perfect statement of the aspirations of the newly wealthy postwar middle classes.

ABOVE In the Bailey Residence, Case Study House No. 21 (1958), Koenig used practical vinyl flooring but defined specific seating areas with carpet. A cooling ribbon of water runs around the house, bordered by terraces that link indoors with out. The steel-framed terraces are made of Bel Air flats, Koenig's trademark brick paver.

LUIS BARRAGÁN

plan and features square and rectangular rooms / large openings without glass and windows linking buildings to landscape / water features

materials rendered brick and concrete / timber beams and staircases

color large areas of brightly washed external wall / small areas internally

furniture Mexican rustic wooden

TOP San Cristobal Stud Farm, Mexico City, 1967–68. Barragán is perhaps Modernism's greatest colorist. His natural pigments, applied to a strong formal geometry, add sensuality and warmth to the austerity of Le Corbusier and the early European Modernists. With a vocabulary deeply rooted in his native Mexico, Barragán plays with large, abstract planes, light and shade, color, water, and nature in his striking designs.

ABOVE Gilardi Residence, Mexico City, 1975–77 (pp. 30–31). The clean lines of the balustrade-free concrete stair, with its wooden treads, combine contemporary Purist geometry and a sympathetic reworking of the pueblo dwelling.

GIO PONTI

plan and features free-flowing / asymmetric and geometric / internal courtyards / inserted terraces at high levels / walls, ceilings, staircases, and roofs appear to float

materials marble floors / ceramic tiles with geometric decoration / painted wooden shutters and screens

color natural / one color plus white

furniture decorated, molded furniture / built-in wooden for specific schemes / brass details / asymmetric and amoeba-like tabletops

ABOVE RIGHT A series of blue-and-white ceramic tiles designed for the Parco dei Principi Hotel in Sorrento, Italy, 1960. Used over large areas on floors and walls, Ponti's subtle optical effects bring an edge to traditional Mediterranean decoration.

TOP Ponti's own home in Milan demonstrates how skillfully he could combine elaborate surface decoration on printed fabric, painted built-in furniture, and colorful folding screens, all of his own design.

ABOVE LEFT The Superleggera Chair, 1955. The manufacturer, Cassina, wanted a light, contemporary chair to suit the smaller apartments of the 1950s, and Ponti produced this classic design, based on the wooden chairs used by local fishermen.

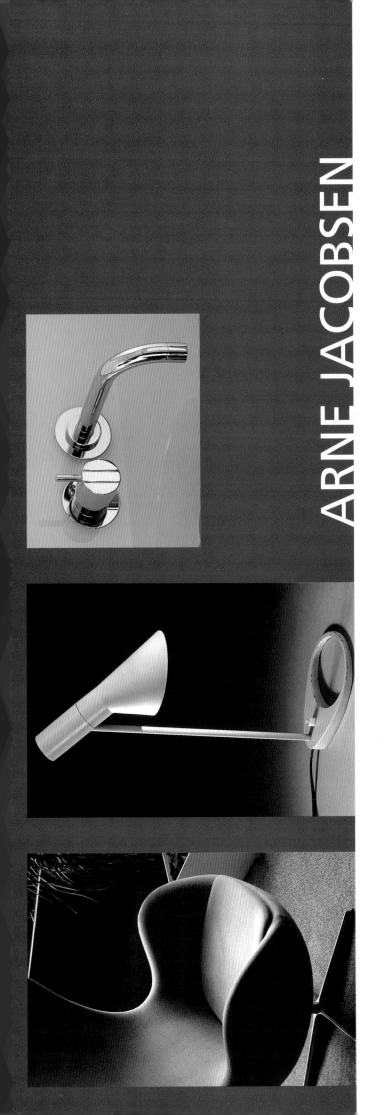

ARNE JACOBSEN

plan and features very varied, including circular houses / open plan / double-height rooms / glass walls / glazed doors

materials wide-ranging, depending on scheme and application / wood

color muted

furniture from molded ply to upholstered fiberglass / organic shapes on steel bases

lighting wide range of own designs

ABOVE LEFT The Egg Chair, 1958: available in fixed and tilting versions

ABOVE CENTER The Visor Lamp, 1957: available in painted metal with an adjustable shade.

ABOVE RIGHT The Vola Taps, 1969: a simple cylinder design with different spouts, available in a variety of combinations

All three remain in production and are now classics of Modern design.

TOP The S.A.S. Hotel lobby, Copenhagen, Denmark (1958), where a flock of Swan chairs is grouped around a central table. The elegant, upholstered, fiberglass chair, on its polished-steel swivel base, was designed specifically for the hotel and is one of Jacobsen's most enduring designs. The color scheme of the hotel, a high-rise block on a podium, is typically muted.

VERNER PANTON

forms extravagant, womblike interiors

materials molded plastics / welded sheet metal / printed Op-Art fabrics / own-design carpets and rugs / surfaces decorated, colored, or faced with relief panels or fabric

color intense / combinations (such as red and purple, or black and white)

furniture foam, wire-frame or cane seating / curvilinear or geometric forms / often exploiting latest technology

TOP A Panton interior—chair, shell lamp, rug, and wall panels. Panton was inspired by the concept of using color "to cause vibrations in the soul" and employed modern industrial techniques to create products in intense shades of red, blue, yellow, and violet. The Panton Chair (1960), the first single cantilevered chair made entirely of plastic, is one of the most famous chair designs of the twentieth century. Taken straight from the mold, it not only eliminated assembly and finishing but was also easier and quieter to stack than chairs with metal bases.

ABOVE Panton's home, Bäsel-Binningen, Switzerland, c. 1973. On the left is Panton's Living Tower, 1968. These sculptural seating towers were designed "to encourage people to use their fantasy and make their surroundings more exciting." To the right is a wall of Panton's mirror sculptures, 1965.

JOHN LAUTNER

plan and features idiosyncratic unique designs, derived from landscape and site / dominant motif or theme

materials taken from site or selected to suit it / wood / plywood / steel / concrete / stone

color natural

furniture built-in / custom-built for projects

lighting varied to suit project / skylights / recessed / concealed

TOP Segel Residence, Malibu, California, 1979. Lautner's characteristic curvilinear concrete forms and use of natural materials combine in a dwelling that seems, viewed from within, to grow cavelike out of the beach itself. The organic curve of the timber-clad ceiling also recalls the sheltering hull of a ship. The furniture, designed by Lautner, is shaped to resemble the stones and boulders on the beach outside, while liberal use of wood on the ceiling and floor warms the interior.

ABOVE Segel Residence, from the beach. Here, its Expressionist outline, wood frame, and grassed-over concrete roof, set amid a boulder-strewn landscape give it the look of driftwood tossed up by the sea.

Beach House, Mornington Peninsula, N.S.W., Australia, by Nik Karalis, 2000

LEFT The raised structure supported on *pilotis* with an entrance ramp to the main living quarters, derives from Le Corbusier's villas of the 1920s. However, the untreated timber exterior, designed to blend into the surrounding landscape, places a different accent on these Modernist features.

OCEAN RETREAT

The Melbourne-based architect Nik Karalis designed this beach house on a rugged peninsula in southeast Australia as a weekend retreat for a city-dwelling family. The house, which fronts the ocean, is surrounded by mountains and sand dunes, and Karalis has effectively built a grandstand for this majestic natural spectacle. Raised above the ground and supported on *pilotis*, the house rests on a concrete platform that projects over shifting sand dunes. "The idea is that the sand will eventually move around it as a natural formation and the house will become part of the landscape."

The exterior of the house is clad in timber to the north, east, and west, while the southern façade is formed of a lightweight skin of glass that reflects the panorama, making the mass of the building disappear. "The house is supposed to mirror the landscape and the clouds, so it doesn't have a presence at all on the south. The big event is the landscape." Karalis wished to re-create the feelings of vulnerability one might experience on this heady Australian peninsula; this intense relationship with nature is fundamental to the design. He felt this house should provide a complete contrast to the family's weekday existence. "In the city we're always covered in safety and warmth. The main requirement of the house was that it be a lot more intimidating, that you felt a lot more exposed."

The house is entered by a ramp along the northern side that leads into a central loggia, dividing the separate living and sleeping wings. This loggia, with its double-fronted doors to the north and full-height sliding glass panels to the south, can be opened on both sides to create a simultaneous indoor/outdoor space. Though Modernist in many of its references—the Corbusier-inspired *pilotis* and ramp, the pavilion-like structure of Mies van der Rohe—the house is strictly twenty-first century in its approach to services and materials. The deep service basement, which stabilizes the building against the wind, contains a vast tank that collects water from the roof and a sewerage processing plant where residue is pumped into an irrigation system. The timber exterior is of unpainted and untreated wood. "Hopefully the building will one day take the color of the bush around it," says Karalis. "Eventually it will gray off to the tea-tree color and it'll become a kind of nonbuilding. If it disintegrates, so be it."

OPPOSITE The central loggia, with its glass doors opening to north and south, both unites the house with the surrounding landscape and divides the sleeping and living quarters.

- As one of *Les Cinq Points d'une Architecture Nouvelle*, Le Corbusier advocated the use of *pilotis* to raise the mass of a house off the ground.
- In Le Corbusier's villas of the 1920s, the main living spaces were accessed by ramps rather than conventional stairs.
- Another of Le Corbusier's five points was the use of loadbearing columns, separate to the walls of a house, thereby allowing an open-plan interior space.

ABOVE The pavilion-like nature of the interior is emphasized by the simplicity of the kitchen incorporated into the main living space. "The kitchen is designed to look like a nonkitchen," explains Karalis. "There's just one long bench and behind it is a storage cupboard that you unfold."

OPPOSITE The freestanding structural steel columns sit entirely within the house, here creating a strong visual counterpoint to the timber skin of the northern façade. The fireplace was designed with a campfire in mind rather than a tame urban hearth, so it is open on three sides.

RIGHT AND BELOW RIGHT The lateral fenestration of the rear façade and gravel drive leading to the house both add a distinct Modernist flavor, with particular reference to Le Corbusier's villas of the 1920s.

OPPOSITE The polished concrete floor below the folded metal stairs was infilled with rivers of steel to give it a pleasingly varied texture. The sand and cement components of the concrete flooring echo the sand and gravel of the drive outside.

MODERNIST REINTERPRETATION

Mark Guard Associates designed this house in west London for a couple of keen Modernists with a young family. The house replaced an existing building constructed in the 1950s, which the couple had originally intended to convert. When it was found impractical to do so, the house was demolished with the exception of the façade, which local residents wished to retain.

The house has, in effect, two façades. The original façade faces onto a private square, but the rear garden also gives onto the street. The rear façade has, therefore, been treated in a formal way with elements that might resemble a front entrance. The large double-height rear window is subdivided with strong horizontal lines, which makes the house appear wider as well as acting as a screen against the facing buildings.

The composition of the rear elevation was inspired by the early Modern Movement—the horizontal muntins and gravel drive making reference to the early work of Le Corbusier. "If you put the house next to a building by Le Corbusier there is no obvious resemblance, but both the windows and the gravel drive were details that stuck in my mind," says Guard. Because of the double aspect of the house, the garden, which is surrounded by white walls, is graveled as a courtyard with a line of pleached pears complementing an existing mature tree.

Guard opted for a Modernist reinterpretation of the traditional town house to maximize all available space whilst blending in with the neighboring buildings. The owners were looking for generous living accommodation, a decent-sized master bedroom, and three additional bedrooms for their children, but they were keen to retain a spacious feel to the interior.

The fire requirements for a four-story town house would normally have resulted in a closed plan, containing a number of rooms on each floor. But here Guard created an entirely different feel by making the space as open as possible and treating the doors as though they were nonexistent. All the doorways were made full height and the doors themselves—flush and painted in the same color as the walls—are held in recesses by electro-magnets, closing only when desired or activated by the fire alarm.

The staircase—in another display of technical virtuosity—is constructed from folded metal plate that has been shotblasted, cleaned, and laquered. The steps are suspended from above, free of the stairwell, except for intermittent small metal rods that pin it to the wall. Although the staircase has been designed to the tightest possible dimensions, the thinness of the steel—only ¼in (6mm) thick—gives the stairwell a spacious feel, and the staircase itself seems light and airy.

The house makes the best use of all available natural light. The second-floor sitting room and study are arranged around a void to the dining room below and are connected to the rear garden by a double-height window. Guard has employed glass extensively throughout the house. Glass floors are used on the bridge over the dining area and to bring light into the children's hallway. The roof above the fourth-floor bathroom is fully glazed.

ABOVE AND OPPOSITE The concealed kitchen units and spacious maple dining table were designed by Mark Guard Associates specifically for the house. The full-height doorways and retracted doors conform to fire regulations but minimize interruptions to the free-flowing space.

- Le Corbusier used lateral fenestration across the façades of many of his villas throughout the 1920s.
- The double-height internal space, overlooked by a balcony, was a key feature of Le Corbusier's Villa la Roche (1923).
- Pierre Koenig often incorporated a full-height wall of storage in his kitchen designs.

The second-floor living space overlooks the double-height dining area from the balcony.

The partly glazed floor of the living space helps to illuminate the

The sinuously curved metal handrail holds the folded-metal

The monochromatic color scheme of the master bedroom adds to the feeling of space.

Within the open-plan master bedroom and connecting bathroom, the broad

The strong geometric form of the bathtub is constructed from large

- In his Glass House (1949), Philip Johnson created a spacious, empty interior that made maximum use of all available light.

- Mies van der Rohe was one of the first architects to use furniture to define an open-plan space.

- During the 1950s and 1960s, Pierre Koenig often used brightly colored furniture within an all-white interior.

MINIMALIST VIEWING PLATFORM

This New York apartment, by interior designers John Barman and Kelly Graham, is a 1980s addition to a typical 1960s glass-box office building. It was, however, to this earlier decade that the designers looked for inspiration.

When Barman and Graham first encountered it, the apartment was already generous and clean-lined, with superb light and wonderful views over the city, but the designers were looking for something much more defined. "We wanted everything to be flat and clean, and very modern. The idea was to create a sense of emptiness, of spaciousness, reminiscent of Philip Johnson's Glass House." They stripped out as much of the existing detailing as possible, removing moldings and taking up the wooden floor and replacing it with polished concrete to create a sleek interior shell. They also flattened out the doors by replacing the handles with stainless-steel inserts made to their own design.

The two-bedroom apartment, with its large living room, dining room, and kitchen is unusual in Manhattan in that its views extend in four directions, giving a spectacular outlook over the city. Barman and Graham have made the most of the panorama, creating a light, open space that acts as a minimalist viewing platform for the skyline, Central Park, and Park Avenue below.

Throughout the apartment a limited color palette has been employed. In the main living space, the designers have used a sharp 1960s palette of black, red, and charcoal set against a plain white backdrop. The sleeping areas are predominantly black, with charcoal carpeting and accents of vibrant red and chrome introduced through the furniture.

In true Modernist manner, furniture plays a crucial role in defining the space. Classic pieces by Arne Jacobsen and Mies van der Rohe that are still in production are intermingled with vintage items from Herman Miller and Knoll. But this is not retro pastiche. The past has been brought very much into the present by reinventing such icons as the Barcelona Chair—normally seen only in black or tan—in brilliant cherry red. Contemporary designs with a 1960s feel—like the Angela Adams red rug—also add an energy that is very much of the moment.

OPPOSITE The stripped-bare, open-plan living space is defined by its simple arrangement of classic Modern pieces in a striking 1960s color scheme. The furniture is grouped and placed for maximum visual impact.

BELOW The Barcelona Chairs by Mies van der Rohe, still in production, have, unusually, been commissioned in cherry red. They sit on a rug by Angela Adams, which is modern but with a 1960s feel.

ABOVE The master bedroom, with its charcoal carpet and draperies, is designed to disappear against the city skyline at night. The Egg Chair and Ottoman are contemporary reproductions of original Modern designs by Arne Jacobsen.

OPPOSITE The table in one corner of the spacious living area is by Eero Saarinen, a furniture designer who worked with Charles and Ray Eames on Case Study House No. 9. This design is still produced by Knoll. The light woolen draperies, which run over all the windows, can be drawn back to reveal the entirety of the frames and the skyline beyond.

- Marcel Breuer and Frank Lloyd Wright both used stone internally as well as externally in their work.
- Strip windows set into timber clad walls were a feature of Richard Neutra's architecture.
- Pierre Koenig often used a single kitchen block with suspended storage in his designs.

BLURRING THE BOUNDARIES

This substantial family house was built on a virgin site in an affluent commuter suburb of New York. The clients—an international businessman working from home and his wife, who commutes daily to the city—were looking for a large family residence that differed radically from the Neocolonial mansions typical of the neighborhood. They envisaged a house that was both dramatic and modern and yet would fit well into the surrounding landscape.

The main concern of the architects, Gilles Depardon and Kathryn Ogawa, was how the building should sit within the local topography. "We didn't want it to stand in nature, we wanted it to feel part of the landscape, not an object within it," explains Depardon. To remain as unobtrusive as possible, the building has been set deep into the sloping ground; viewed from the front, the house appears as a long, low box that merges almost seamlessly with the surrounding woodland.

Nestling between two rocky outcrops, the 8,000 square feet (745m²) property incorporates six bedrooms and a home office, as well as an extremely generous reception space. L-shaped in plan, the building consists of a single-story wing, which houses the bedrooms and the office, and a main living space to the rear that is split over two levels. The site for this home was chosen specifically for its pond, which sits at the bottom of the slope to the rear of the house. This feature became a focal point of the design; the double-height windows that extend across the majority of the rear façade allow an uninterrupted view.

Using traditional building materials in a Modern way, Depardon and Ogawa built the house of a local Vermont stone. This stone, known as Dover, was cut square and combined with large expanses of plate glass to create a striking façade. This wall treatment was continued inside the house to give a sense of continuity from exterior to interior; local stone-wall builders were used to create various features within the house, such as the chimney wall that provides a focal point for the main living space. Similarly, the stone flooring used in the lobby is carried across the exterior courtyard and into the dining room beyond, thereby blurring the boundaries between indoors and out.

Throughout the house, built-in furniture, such as the kitchen block with suspended storage, has been combined with vintage and contemporary pieces. The architects made their selection of 1960s furniture from a former IBM office building that was being cleared; they combined these original Knoll pieces with furniture and fixtures from other designers, including Alvar Aalto and Arne Jacobsen, to create a cohesive Modernist interior.

ABOVE LEFT The long line of windows across the timber-clad front elevation are reminiscent of Neutra's strip windows, which the Californian architect used on service areas and sides of buildings. Here, they fulfil a practical as well as aesthetic function, helping to create cooling cross ventilation.

ABOVE RIGHT The original 1960s furniture by Knoll, used throughout the house, was rescued by the architects from a former IBM office building. Here, the brown three-seater sofa and the chair at the window are both vintage pieces given a new lease of life.

OPPOSITE On the rear elevation, a narrow band of windows subdivides the two larger panes of glass, keeping out mosquitoes but letting in cooling breezes without obscuring the view.

THIS PAGE The two-story, open-plan living area, floored entirely in Brazilian walnut, is truly Modernist in its sense of light, airy, interlocking interior space.

OPPOSITE The continuation of polished stone flooring from the living areas across an open courtyard helps to blur the boundaries between interior and exterior. The dining table and chairs viewed in the farthest room are by Alvar Aalto.

The house, built of Dover stone, is both part of nature and a
focus on it. Indoors, this integration of the natural and the
man-made is continued in the combination of polished stone
and wood with steel and plate glass.

- In his early Modernist villas, Le Corbusier frequently used internal balconies and high openings in interior walls.
- Polished wood walls are a feature of Mies van der Rohe's interiors.
- Richard Neutra used frameless corner windows in his designs.

BELOW The sleek, frameless corner windows, seen here from inside the third-story bathroom, are also an element of Neutra's architecture and form an almost imperceptible barrier between inside and out. The cool marble surface surrounding the sink further blurs this boundary as it echoes the snowy landscape visible beyond the rear of the house. The Vola Taps are an original design by Arne Jacobsen.

OPPOSITE A narrow, vertical strip window, set deep into the exterior wall to the right side of the fireplace, demonstrates the depth of the stonework and solidity of the building. Viewed from inside the main living area, it highlights the uniform treatment of walls internally and externally, as both can be viewed simultaneously from this particular vantage point.

TOP AND ABOVE Although the sofa is not, in fact, built in, it fits and fills its intended home as though it were. The stepped shelving is Modernist in origin, as is the internal glass window, which negates the solidity of the wall.

The pale suede upholstered headboard, stepped integrated bedside table, and indulgent fur throw are all decorative details found in the work of the architect and furniture designer Eileen Gray.

Long, built-in working elements that emphasized the lines of the room, such as this workspace shelving, were a common Modernist motif. Similarly, lacquerwork was a popular 1930s finish and a trademark of Eileen Gray.

The central pillar, suspended staircase, steel balustrade, and tubular-steel furniture all originated in the machine aesthetic of Le Corbusier and can be viewed in many of his villas of the 1920s.

COOL CITY COMFORT

This Victorian four-story house in a garden square in West London had been gutted and restructured before it was taken on by its present owner. The structural renovation had introduced certain key elements beloved by the Modern Movement: the Corbusier-inspired double-height extension, with its latticework of black steel, successfully integrates indoors with out, and the open staircase, with its wooden treads and diagonal steel handrail, floats graphically against the plain white walls.

The owner has furnished the house very much within the Modernist aesthetic, the emphasis being far more on form and structure than on decoration, with a crisply chic use of line and geometrical pattern. Furniture has been kept clean-lined and uncluttered, ornament reduced to a minimum.

The built-in furnishings echo those adopted by Modern Movement designers to save space and create a more harmonious effect. Here, the elongated red lacquer desk, with its accompanying shelving, cleverly emphasizes the horizontal lines of the drawing room. In the bedroom, the interesting juxtaposition of the stepped bedside table and the screen behind the bed unites practicality and geometry.

The palette in this West London house is a richly sophisticated spectrum of deep reds, black, and blues that works particularly effectively against the purity of the white walls. The fur throw and suede headboard—materials not found in the work of the more austere pioneers of the Modern Movement—add a sensuous and more feminine note.

LEFT The new double-height extension, added to the rear of this period property, demonstrates a central tenet of Modernist architecture. The glazed rear elevation and roof, supported by structural steel frames, remove the necessity for load-bearing walls thereby facilitating the free-flowing space between the first-floor dining area and second-floor living room.

- In his early Modernist villas, Le Corbusier combined free-flowing space with an internal balcony.

- Le Corbusier placed traditional upholstered armchairs within a Modernist interior.

- Le Corbusier was one of the first architects to use a suspended open-plan staircase with complementary steel balustrade.

OPPOSITE Here, in what was once the formal drawing room of a Victorian stucco house, one clearly sees the influence of the Modernist aesthetic. The large expanse of plate glass breaking down the barrier between indoors and out, the unornamented furniture, and the clever interplay of geometries are all ideas that originated with the International Style.

MODERN YET CONTEMPORARY

- Luis Barragán has made solid blocks of strong color used on the internal walls a key feature of his work.
- Alvar Aalto incorporated a screen-printed fabric, patterned with regular dashes, designed by his wife into his interiors.
- Marcel Breuer introduced the use of wall-mounted storage into his designs.

This remodeling of the Swedish ambassador's residence in Berlin involved a radical transformation of an existing building dating from the 1940s. Much of the original structure was erased while a historic garden, by the celebrated German garden designer Herta Hammerbacher, was protected and enhanced. The original building, by Wilhelm Gumbertz, was given a full upper-floor addition, as well as a new dining room, a sunroom extension to one of the existing drawing rooms, and a professional kitchen.

The entire first floor is given over to the ambassador's official work and entertaining. Designed primarily for formal functions, it contains three inter-linking drawing rooms and a large dining room. The newly extended second floor houses the ambassador's private five-bedroom apartment and two smaller apartments for servants and guests.

The outstanding garden was the main focus of the design, both externally and internally. All the drawing rooms and the dining room have now been given direct access to the south-facing terrace, where much of the entertaining takes place. The new dining room has been cantilevered from and over the retaining walls in the garden to minimize any damage.

The architects, Lasse Vretblad and Louise Levander, chose to erase almost all of the decorative features of the original design, but have retained significant proportions of the old masonry, making most of their additions in glass. A large proportion of this glass has been screen printed for sun protection on the south side and privacy on the north.

While recognizing the need to accommodate the traditional layout and functions of the residence, Claesson Koivisto Rune, the young architectural practice responsible for the interior design of the first-floor drawing rooms, wanted to create something both Modern and contemporary. The need for guests to be able to move effortlessly through the reception rooms dictated an entirely open plan. The architects chose portals rather than doors to mark the transition between rooms and a color scheme that unites the interior.

The color scheme was based on a natural spectrum matched to pebbles taken from a Swedish beach; the palette used in this interior ranges from cappuccino, through gray to white. Besides unifying room with room, the color was intended to link house with garden. Color has been used in blocks—after the manner of Luis Barragán—with lightest colors facing the garden and gradually moving to darker, more shadowy, gray walls at the core of the building.

Materials are both traditional and modern. The flooring throughout is a white-stained, contemporary veined oak, much of the detailing is in walnut, a wood that the architects felt represented something solid, expensive, and appropriate. The walnut and the specially commissioned range of contemporary furniture by fifty modern Swedish designers, works as a distinctive contrast to the paler floor plane.

ABOVE Much of the new glass walling, which forms the exterior skin of the building, has been screen printed for privacy and sun protection.

BELOW The architects had to take into account both the demand for free circulation between the reception rooms and the need to match seating at the dining table with that in the drawing rooms. The walnut detailing provides a contrast to the paler oak floor. The color scheme throughout is in a range of neutrals, inspired by pebbles on a Swedish beach.

OPPOSITE The south-facing garden frontage with its new dining room, sunroom, and terrace, unites the remodelled house with the historic garden.

Here, in the most intimate of the three reception rooms, the interior architects have used strong blocks of color, after the work of Luis Barragán. Both the view into the garden and access to it have been facilitated at every point.

MODERNIST IN INSPIRATION

This apartment in New York was designed for a client who wanted a very modern space, that would make the best use of his exceptional seventh-floor river views, while providing generous living and working accommodation.

Architects Gilles Depardon and Kathryn Ogawa decided to deconstruct the existing conventionally arranged two-bedroom apartment, taking down all the walls and opening up the whole into a single space, enclosing only the bedroom and exercise room. The living space itself is Modernist in its inspiration, using varying levels to define changes in function, such as working and dining. It also employs the Japanese technique of borrowed views—in which the background takes precedence over the foreground—to draw the eye toward the exceptional view.

In order to bring maximum light into the east-facing bedroom at the back of the apartment, the designers enclosed the bedroom in steel-framed glass doors. These doors operate on pivots; when open, they unite the private space of the bedroom with the public living space beyond. The doors themselves are composed of two layers of glass interlaid with a translucent Japanese paper, which emphasizes their screenlike quality.

The light and simplicity of the space have been enhanced by painting the entire apartment white and screening the windows in simple white roller shades. Materials are a neutral blend of traditional wood with modern glass and steel. The furniture, chosen by the architects, is a combination of clean-lined contemporary pieces and vintage Knoll.

RIGHT AND FAR RIGHT The master bedroom is painted white and furnished with a mixture of built-in architect-designed units, contemporary Italian pieces, and vintage Knoll. The flooring is of painted wood.

OPPOSITE The minimalist kitchen, with its built-in wooden units and Koenig-like hanging shelving, has been deliberately kept small and neat to complement the client's hectic lifestyle.

- **Richard Neutra used differing levels to define areas and their function within an open-plan space.**
- **Mies van der Rohe used a single type of wood to completely finish one wall.**
- **Folding steel-framed doors were used by Pierre Koenig in his designs.**
- **For all his interior schemes, Richard Neutra designed built-in furniture to achieve a unified look.**

THIS PAGE The east-facing bedroom enclosed behind steel-framed glass doors, which maintain privacy while introducing the maximum amount of light.

OPPOSITE The pure-white open space is layered to define the varying functions of different areas and to draw the eye directly to the river views.

ABOVE AND ABOVE RIGHT The house is clad in a popular local material, galvanized zinc, which lends a muted reflective quality. The windows match front and back.

RELAXED OPEN-PLAN SPACE

The Canadian furniture designer Neils Bendtsen designed this house for his own family to replace an existing house on a hillside site in suburban Vancouver, just a five-minute walk from the Pacific. Neils and his wife, Nancy, were looking for "something real to live in"—a clean, modern space that would make the best use of their wonderful ocean views and south-facing garden whilst comfortably accommodating themselves, their three young daughters, and a live-in nanny. "We wanted an informal family home, with a playroom and a kitchen that overlooked the view— so I could see it when I was standing chopping vegetables—plus somewhere my husband could work at home near to, but not part of, the family chaos," explains Nancy.

Their three-story house is not large—just 3,000 square feet (900m²)—but manages to comfortably contain five bedrooms, four bathrooms, and a playroom, as well as a generous open-plan kitchen, living room, and study. The entrance, on the lower-ground floor, is attached to a double garage and leads to the playroom and a private bedroom and bathroom. The first floor is given over to the open-plan multi-functional living space, while the four remaining bedrooms and three bathrooms are on the second floor.

The Bendtsens were inspired, when designing the house, both by the relaxed open-plan spaces of Charles and Ray Eames and those of the Australian architect Glen Murcott. The house was constructed from concrete and steel, then clad in galvanized zinc, a popular local industrial material, which gives the exterior a muted reflective quality as well as an attractive powdery silver colour. The many windows—which match north and south—make the house extremely light and are designed to supply a cooling cross breeze in the hot summer months. A deck runs the full length of the south-facing ocean frontage, as well as on part of the northern façade, providing more or less continuous access to the outdoors.

This intimate relationship with the landscape has been emphasized still further by painting all the interior walls white. "We initially tried color, but there is so much happening outside it simply didn't work," comments Bendtsen. The space is both minimally and comfortably furnished with pieces both by the owner and by such leading designers as Alvar Aalto and Charles and Ray Eames.

TOP AND ABOVE The open-plan first-floor living space is furnished with classic Modern pieces such as the table by Alvar Aalto, the armchair by Charles Eames, and the sofa by owner Neils Bendtsen. The walls throughout are painted white; the flooring is maple.

ABOVE AND RIGHT The concrete-encased staircase of purple heartwood suspended on steel brackets slices through the main living space, but the open treads leave the view clear.

- In his Case Study House No. 8 (1949), Charles Eames used a structural framework and steel-framed windows which formed a grid within a grid.
- Double-height living spaces are a key feature of Le Corbusier's interiors.
- Alvar Aalto incorporated an office area with a wall of books into his designs.
- Pierre Koenig designed a central kitchen block for many of his interiors.

OPPOSITE The clean angles of the banisterless staircase can be found originally in the work of Luis Barragán. The floor-to-ceiling, sliding ply doors, bought from an industrial supplier, introduce a machine aesthetic and contribute to the feeling of space. The flooring, too, is a unifying element. Reclaimed strip maple was used throughout the three-story height, except in the kitchen and dining area.

OPENING UP THE HOUSE

From the outside, this yellow-brick Victorian row house in East London looks precisely as it did when it was built more than 150 years ago. Inside, however, it has been entirely deconstructed and reassembled by its current owner, Andrew Weaving. "One of the reasons we found the house attractive," comments Weaving, "was that, when we bought it, it had been gutted both in the 1950s and 1970s and all the original features removed. We therefore felt free to rip everything out and start again."

Weaving wanted to create something much lighter, simpler, and more open—essentially something more Modern. "I wanted to create the idea of the house as one room on several levels." To this end, Weaving took down many walls and put up in their place sliding walls and folding partitions, inspired by ideas found in the work of Le Corbusier and Richard Neutra.

The original rickety dogleg staircase, which made an immediate impact when entering through the front door, was also repositioned to form a dramatic new entrance hall. The direction of the staircase was reversed so that the additional area, previously boxed in as a cupboard, could be incorporated into the hall to provide extra floor space. The bold, simple zigzag of this new staircase derives from the work of Luis Barragán.

Weaving has incorporated Modernist detailing throughout the house. In the living room, for example, the linear storage built by Weaving himself was taken from the horizontal cabinets of Marcel Breuer, while the simplified outline of the fireplace can be found in the work of Richard Meier. Elsewhere in the house Weaving looked to the California School: the kitchen design with its island layout derives from Pierre Koenig, while the folding screens that subdivide the kitchen from the hall are a device originally employed by Richard Neutra.

In order to enhance the feeling of unity and space, the palette throughout the house has been kept to a Modernist spectrum of neutrals. "We originally painted the hall white and all the partition walls in quite strong colors, but the bright colors seemed too harsh against the white. Because the building is old and the angles between the walls and the ceiling not quite straight, the strong contrasts merely emphasized the faults." Now soft stones, creams, and taupes sit more comfortably against the white.

Furniture is important to Weaving. As the owner of Century, a leading vintage furniture shop in London, he has a particular interest in twentieth-century design. Much of the furniture in his own home is by the leading contemporary British designer Jasper Morrison, but this is intermingled with key vintage pieces by George Nelson, Charles and Ray Eames, and the British designer Robin Day.

BELOW When designing the kitchen floor, Weaving was inspired by a book on Marcel Breuer's work at the Bauhaus and by a visit to Le Corbusier's Villa La Roche. The 6-inch (15cm) quarry tiles have been laid to form a decorative pattern in shades of black, white, and brown.

The tiled floor defines the lower level of the kitchen and dining area. The shop-bought maple units were customized with Formica worksurfaces and painted medium-density fiberboard edging to resemble the kitchen designs of Pierre Koenig.

The folding-screen doors, which mark the transition from entrance hall to kitchen and from kitchen to dining room, were made by Weaving in polished medium-density fiberboard after those used by Richard Neutra. The wall clock is by George Nelson; the stools are by Jasper Morrison.

BELOW The unity of the space is aided by repeating the color scheme of the lower floor. The lighting in the headboard is original 1960s, the bedcover by American designer Judy Ross.

OPPOSITE The glass brick walling, set at a 45-degree angle to the house, both defines the second bathroom and illuminates an otherwise dark space. "The glass bricks are originally from the 1930s, but I wanted them to serve a contemporary purpose rather than just acting as a decorative pastiche,' explains Weaving. "Fortunately, here, we were able to use them to bring light into a landing that would otherwise have been windowless."

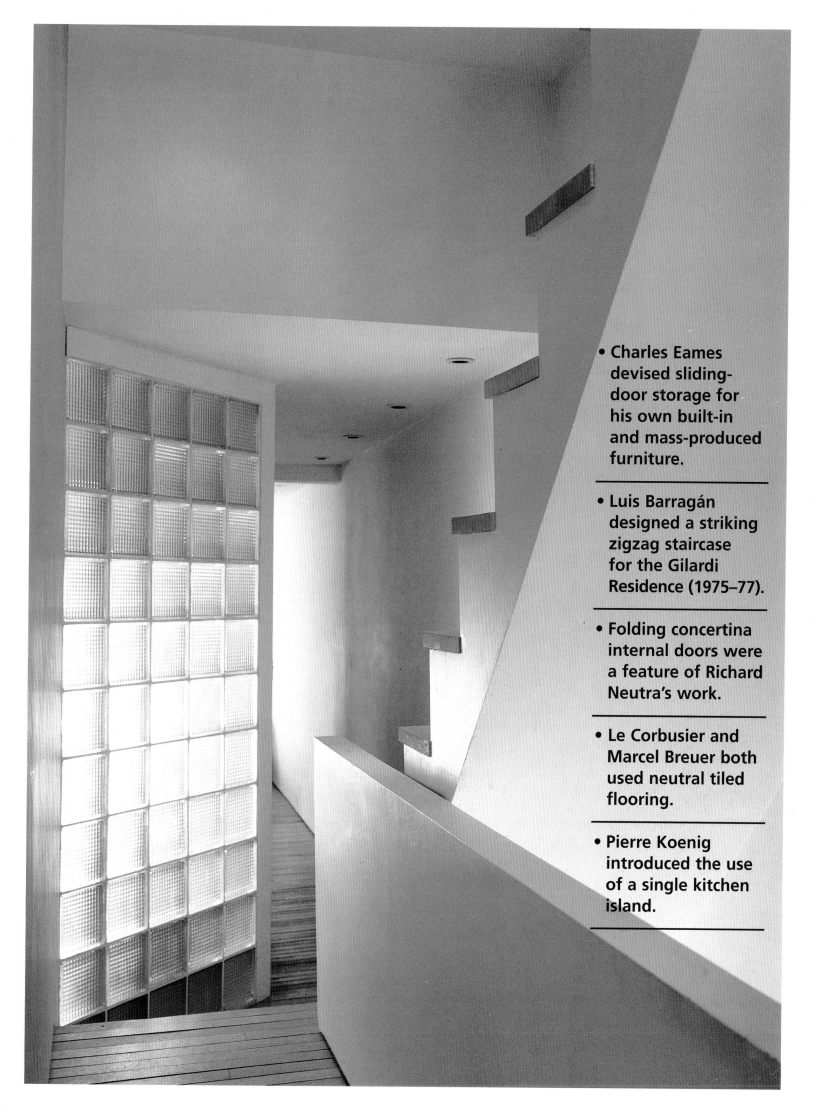

- Charles Eames devised sliding-door storage for his own built-in and mass-produced furniture.

- Luis Barragán designed a striking zigzag staircase for the Gilardi Residence (1975–77).

- Folding concertina internal doors were a feature of Richard Neutra's work.

- Le Corbusier and Marcel Breuer both used neutral tiled flooring.

- Pierre Koenig introduced the use of a single kitchen island.

LEFT The rooftop bulkhead, of mahogany and copper, was designed to be invisible from the street. It provides protected viewing in inclement weather and a sculptural presence on the roof.

REINVENTED SPACE

- **Lautner designed an angled roof-top elevation for the Walstrom Residence (1969).**

- **Walter Gropius made a zigzag staircase the central feature of his Lincoln Residence (1938).**

- **Pierre Koenig devised the functional kitchen block as a key feature of his Modernist interiors.**

This apartment, designed for a banker with a keen interest in motor racing, was conceived as the ultimate bachelor pad. On the tenth floor of a converted industrial building in Tribeca, it looks out over the Hudson River and down on one of the city's few parks. Its wraparound windows, facing south and west, provide particularly good light as well as outstanding views.

Though the apartment had already been converted from industrial use, the architects, Sager Wimer Coombe, reinvented the space, retaining certain significant original features, while creating a spacious 2,500 square feet (750m²), open-plan contemporary residence. The most radical change they made, however, was to break the building's shell through to the roof space above, reinforcing the apartment's relationship to the landscape, and introducing a dramatic central staircase, which became a defining element of the design.

The staircase divides the open-plan space into three discrete zones, for eating, cooking, and sitting, while the more private functions of the apartment—the bedroom, bathrooms, and laundry room—inhabit the perimeter. Constructed using steel plate on site, this staircase wraps around a sandblasted glass panel etched with decorative ovals emphasizing its dual function as a sculpture in its own right, as well as a functional means of access.

At the point where the staircase meets the roof it gives out onto a protected bulkhead in mahogany and copper, which, in order to meet local sightline regulations, needed to be invisible from the street. The bulkhead acts both as a protected viewing platform and as a transitional space between indoors and out. The roof terrace is seen by the architects as a counterpoint to the living space below; while the latter provides a private world to look out unperceived, the former is a public arena, where the viewer becomes visible, like "an actor on a stage."

The architects wished to retain the original character of the building—the tallest wood-frame structure still in existence in New York—and incorporated its industrial steel plates and columns into the design undisguised. Elsewhere they worked in a rich mixture of natural and industrial materials—mahogany, copper, steel, granite, cherrywood, and black-stained oak—to create a clean, contemporary palette of neutrals.

The furniture, chosen by the architects, includes some vintage pieces—such as the distinctive George Nelson bubble lamps—and other built-in elements of the architect's own design.

The central staircase, made of steel and sandblasted glass, subdivides the open-plan public living space whilst also serving as a striking piece of contemporary sculpture.

The view from the rooftop terrace shows the transition from the intimate space of the apartment to the full blast of the New York skyline.

The sculptural zigzag of the staircase draws the eye upwards to the viewing platform and across into the functional kitchen area.

EVER-SHIFTING COLLAGE

Successful industrial designer Karim Rashid converted this apartment from the dereliction of 100-hundred-year-old stables in the fashionable Chelsea district of Manhattan. Taking the 665 square feet (200m²) of dark and neglected space, he opened up the building into a brilliant, white loft to provide a versatile backdrop for his pop-colored furniture, lighting, tableware, and gadgets. The clean, bright, boxlike apartment is now a neutral but dynamic space that plays home to an ever-shifting collage of Rashid's high-energy furniture and products. "I make little groupings of whatever is here at the time. Prototypes are constantly moving in and out of the space."

In order to bring as much light into the apartment as possible, Rashid knocked a series of floor-to-ceiling windows into the main street façade. At the rear of the apartment, he inserted a single large window, giving what he calls a "Milan View" of the alley below.

To maximize the sense of openness and drama, Rashid contained the services—the vestibule, bathrooms, and utility room—in a block along one wall, while taking advantage of two existing I-beams in the main living space to define the open-plan kitchen. Here, he lowered the ceiling height and ran two uninterrupted parallel lines of stainless-steel and plastic laminate units between the beams to create a more intimate horizontal counterpoint to the soaring vertical space around.

Architecturally, Rashid's design owes its heritage to the California School, in particular the work of Richard Neutra. His product design, however, is rooted in Italy, where as a student in the 1980s, he encountered the decorative, colorful plastic laminates of the design group Memphis. Rashid's own vivid, organic designs are drawn entirely on the computer, which, he feels, has liberated him to break new barriers in color, form and material. "Objects and space should speak about the moment in which we live."

ABOVE The neutral living space is the perfect backdrop for Rashid's vividly colored furniture. The circular Omni sofa is intended to redefine the way we interact. "Usually," says Rashid, "you have one long couch facing-off with the TV. I wanted something more casual that encourages sitting in a different way and stimulates conversation."

OPPOSITE Rashid groups together whatever furniture is passing through the space—here his Planar sofa and Aura glass coffee table demonstrate the versatility of the computer-generated curve when applied to product design.

THIS PAGE The single-run kitchen is made from stainless steel and laminate. With uniform floor and wall units, the kitchen is designed as two uninterrupted parallel lines.

OPPOSITE Two of Rashid's distinctive vases sit on a dining table made from his own "morphscape" laminate. Generated by computer, the design is inspired by Op Art of the 1960s.

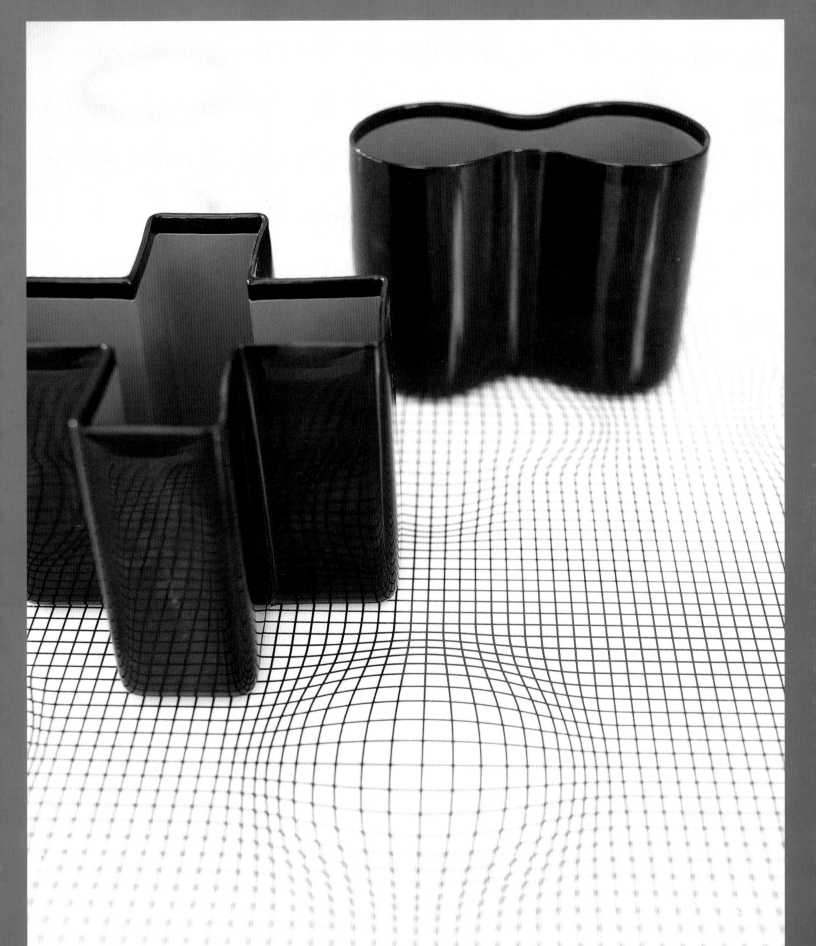

- Pierre Koenig used highly polished, synthetic flooring in an all-white interior for his Case Study House No. 21 (1958).
- Gio Ponti frequently decorated the flat surfaces of floors and furniture with highly abstract patterns.
- Verner Panton designed integral curved seating units during the 1970s in vivid colorways.

THIS PAGE The bathroom—in luminous primaries—continues the theme of stainless steel and laminate. The vertical, linear, incandescent lighting is inspired by the sculpture of contemporary artist Dan Flavin.

OPPOSITE A corner of the main living area, where Rashid's organic forms translated into glass and fabric work together in brilliant harmony.

- John Lautner constructed houses on and into rock.
- Pierre Koenig designed large living spaces connected by a courtyard, with vast expanses of glass to maximize views.
- Charles Eames championed the use of prefabricated, readily available materials in the construction of his own home.

OPPOSITE Viewed from the street below, the house is a dramatic form nestling into the surrounding landscape. Built using standard parts, such as cement boards and aluminum-framed windows, bought direct from a builder's catalog, the house makes a stylish yet cost-effective home.

BELOW The dining room, with table designed by architects Escher GuneWardena, forms part of a long, continuous living space with windows on three sides of the house. The partially-glazed terraces provides an interior/exterior space with extraordinary views of Pasadena below.

180-DEGREE OUTLOOK

The Jamie Residence, by Los Angeles–based architects Escher GuneWardena, sits within the Californian tradition of the technically innovative, moderately priced family home, uniting an intense involvement with nature with a relaxed attitude to daily living.

The house—on a steep and difficult site in the prosperous suburb of Pasadena—was built for a professional couple and their young child. The clients wanted a three-bedroom house with a study and playroom as well as more formal living and dining areas. But their greatest concern was that best use was made of the dramatic panorama, which includes views of Pasadena below, the San Gabriel mountains to the east, and the San Rafael hills to the west.

The architects, working within a relatively constricted budget, wished to create a house which managed to be both visually exciting and elegant, and ecologically sensitive to the water-deprived environment. Their imaginative solution obviated the need for huge retaining walls and has minimized the structure's contact with the ground. Two large concrete piers carry two steel beams spanning a 84-foot (25m) length, which in turn support the wood-framed house dramatically above. The two piers are the only elements to meet the ground, permitting maximum water drainage and allowing the natural landscaping to continue beneath the house. Access to the house is by a bridge that connects it to the road on the uphill side of the property.

The plan is designed to maintain views from all of the rooms, and both the positioning of the windows and the arrangement of the living space have been dictated by this requirement. The windows—no longer simply defining elements in an elevation—have been carefully inserted to frame the view, thereby enhancing the contact with nature and enlarging the sense of space within. The living room, dining room, outdoor deck, kitchen, and family room are all interconnected, and create a continuous space with a 180-degree outlook over the cityscape and landscape.

The house was furnished by the architects using their own-design furniture intermingled with contemporary pieces they felt to be in keeping with the clean lines and relaxed, modern feel of the house.

1950s... FLAMBOYANTLY RESTYLED

This seaside house in Miami, owned by rock star Lenny Kravitz, was originally built in the 1950s but has been entirely, and flamboyantly, restyled by designer Michael Cyzsz, director of the Oregon-based firm Architropolis.

The house was originally significantly smaller, and Czysz, restricted by planning regulations, was unable to enlarge it. Instead he made considerable internal alterations, including roofing over an outdoor area to create the 2,000 square feet (600m²) living room. "Many of the exterior curves were original to the house, but we cleaned up the elevation and extended the inside to outside," says Czysz. The austere, curving, gray concrete façade is now finished with a stainless-steel gate and a purple laminated front door.

Both internally and externally, the house is a dramatic marriage of retro and twenty-first century, making particular reference to the work of Danish designer Verner Panton in its luminous walls and molded multicolored furniture. The use of color and materials is eclectic and dramatic. Kravitz demanded "white fur" and "bubbles", so Czysz upholstered walls and furnishings with white fake fur, and lined the living room ceiling and walls, as well as those of the outdoor swimming pool, with silvered Op Art bubbles.

An equal lack of restraint has been applied throughout—the living room's expansive curved bar is sculpted in stitched white patent leather, the centerpiece sofa is 40 feet (12m) of shrieking tangerine, whilst an arched ceiling of celestial blue mirror tiles surmounts the bed. The lighting is as brilliant and unnatural as a stage set, with lurid shades of psychedelic red and blue making the house more reminiscent of a nightclub than an intimate personal space. Light glares out from the ceilings, from the walls, even from the bar, and is dazzlingly reflected back in the myriad of silver bubble mirrors.

The house is fantastical, too, in its James Bond–like attachment to gadgetry. Controlled from a computer installed in the sofa, sliding red Plexiglas doors guard the entrance to the living room, while Kravitz's blue-mirrored bedroom is equipped with a video screen in the sandblasted bedhead, providing underwater coverage of the swimming pool.

ABOVE The minimalist, gray concrete façade is punctured by the entrance of sandblasted security glass. The vintage Thunderbird, as with Pierre Koenig's carefully styled automobiles, sets the tone.

ABOVE The dramatic, vast living room, now half the area of the house, was created by roofing over part of the garden. It features a glass wall overlooking the swimming pool and Miami's Biscayne Bay.

RIGHT The Heavy Petting Room, with its laminated plastic portal and undulating multicolored sections, is Czysz's homage to Verner Panton, giving views of the living room, with its white patent-leather bar.

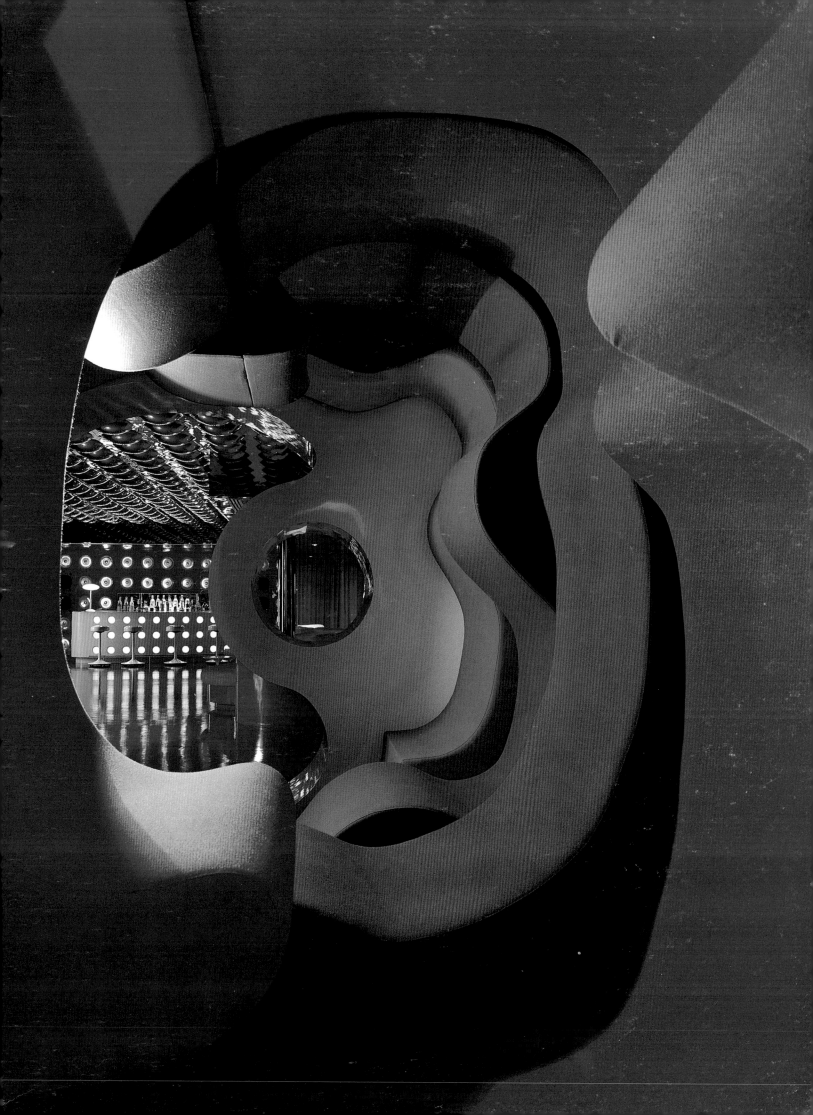

The vast living room is decorated with a 40-foot- (12m-) long sofa, a 4-inch- (10cm-) deep shag pile rug, a stainless-steel pool table, and a bar bound in white patent leather. The tulip tables are by Eero Saarinen.

- Throughout the 1960s, Verner Panton designed interiors using vivid color schemes, living towers, and wall reliefs.
- Pierre Koenig incorporated walls of glass into his interior designs.
- Chrome columns were used by Mies van der Rohe as both a functional and decorative element in his architecture.
- John Lautner designed built-in curved seating for his interiors.

The white fur tunnel and metal catwalk lead to an 007-style sliding red Plexiglas door that opens onto the living space. The stainless-steel foyer beyond is studded with a myriad of incandescent lightbulbs.

Op Art–inspired, silvered acrylic bubbles surround the outdoor pool, reflecting and refracting the water, sky, and swimmers.

RESOURCES

Modern architecture and design

Books

Bauhaus: Fifty Years, Royal Academy, 1968.

Benton, Charlotte, *A Different World: Émigré Architects in Britain*, RIBA, 1995.

Bingham, Neil and Weaving, Andrew, *Modern Retro: Living with Mid-century Modern Style*, Ryland, Peters & Small, 2000.

Copplestone, Trewin, *Twentieth-century World Architecture*, Brian Todd Publishing, 1991.

Cygelman, Adele and Glomb, David, *Palm Springs Modern: Houses in the California Desert*, Rizzoli International Publications, 1999.

Dietsch, Deborah K., *Classic Modern: Mid-century Modern at Home*, Simon & Schuster, 2000.

Frampton, Kenneth, *Modern Architecture: A Critical History*, Thames and Hudson, 1992.

Frampton, Kenneth and Larkin, David, *American Masterworks: The Twentieth-century House*, Rizzoli International Publications, 1995.

Jackson, Lesley, *Contemporary*, Phaidon, 1994.

Khan, Hasan-Uddin, *International Style: Modernist Architecture from 1925 to 1965*, Taschen, 1998.

Kirsh, Karin, *The Weissenhofsiedlung*, Rizzoli International Publications, 1989.

Knobel, Lance, *Faber Guide to Twentieth-century Architecture in Britain and Northern Europe*, Faber & Faber, 1985.

McCarter, Robert et al, *Twentieth-century House: by Frank Lloyd Wright, Charles and Ray Eames and Alvar Aalto*, Phaidon, 1999.

McCoy, Esther, *Case Study House 1945–62*, Hennessey & Ingalls, 1977.

McMillan, Elizabeth, *Beach Houses from Malibu to Laguna*, Rizzoli International Publications, 1994.

Meadmore, Clement et al, *The Modern Chair: Classic Designs by Thonet, Breuer, Le Corbusier, Eames and Others*, Dover Publications, 1997.

Nelson, George and Wright, Henry, *Tomorrow's House*, Simon & Schuster, 1945.

Pearson, Clifford et al, *Modern American Houses: Four Decades of Award-winning Design in Architectural Record*, Harry N. Abrams, 1996.

Saeks, Diane Dorrans, *California Interiors*, Taschen, 1999.

Schezen, Roberto et al, *Private Architecture: Masterpieces of the Twentieth Century*, Monacelli Press, 1998.

Sembach, Klaus-Jurgen, *Into the Thirties*, Thames & Hudson, 1986.

Serraino, Pierluigi and Shulman, Julius, *Modernism Rediscovered*, Taschen, 2000.

Sharp, Dennis et al, *Twentieth-century Classics: by Walter Gropius, Le Corbusier and Louis Khan*, Phaidon, 1999.

Smith, Elizabeth A.T., *Blueprints for Modern Living: History and Legacy of the Case Study Houses*, MIT Press, 1998.

Snibbe, Patricia M. & Richard W., *The New Modernist in World Architecture*, McGraw-Hill, 1999.

Stoller, Ezra, *Modern Architecture*, Harry N. Abrams, 1990.

Thirties, Arts Council of Great Britain, 1979.

Turner, Judith, *Photographs of Five Architects*, Rizzoli International Publications, 1980.

Weston, Richard, *Modernism*, Phaidon, 1996.

Yorke, F.R.S., *The Modern House*, Architectural Press, 1934.

Further information

Bauhaus Archive Museum of Design
Klingelhöferstrasse 14, 10785 Berlin, Germany
Tel: +49 (0)30 254 00 20
bauhaus.de
Permanent collection, including work by Gropius, Breuer and Mies van der Rohe, temporary exhibitions, lectures and workshops

Chicago Architecture Foundation (CAF)
224 South Michigan Avenue, Chicago, IL 60604
Tel: (312) 922 3432
architecture.org
Architectural tours, exhibitions, lectures and special events

Documentation and Conservation of the Modern Movement (DOCOMOMO)
Delft University of Technology, Berlageweg 1, 2628 CR Delft, Netherlands
Tel: +31 (15) 278 8755
Fax: +31 (15) 278 8750
e-mail: docomomo@bk.tudelft.nl
docomomo.com
Research, preservation and annual newsletter with branches worldwide

The Great Buildings Collection
greatbuildings.com
Online directory of architects and buildings

International Architectural Database
archinform.net
Online directory of architects and buildings

Royal Institute of British Architects (RIBA)
66 Portland Place, London W1B 1AD, England
Tel: +44 (0)20 7580 5533
Fax: +44 (0)20 7255 1541
e-mail: admin@inst.riba.org
architecture.com
Archive, exhibitions, lectures and directory of recommended practices in Australia, the UK and the US

Society of Architectural Historians
1365 North Astor Street, Chicago, IL 60610
Tel: (312) 573 1365
Fax: (312) 573 1141
sah.org
Architectural tours, research and preservation with branches throughout the US

20th Century Society
70 Cowcross Street, London EC1M 6EJ, England
Tel: +44 (0)20 7250 3857
e-mail: administrator@c20society.demon.co.uk
c20society.demon.co.uk
Architectural tours

Vitra Design Museum
Charles Eames strasse 1, D-79576 Weil am Rhein, Germany
Tel: +49 (7)621 702 35 78
Fax: +49 (7)621 702 31 46
Kopenhagerstrasse 58, D-10437 Berlin/ Prenzlauer Berg, Germany
Tel: +49 (0)30 473 777 0
Fax: +49 (0)30 473 777 20
e-mail: info@design-museum.de
vitra.com

Alvar Aalto

Houses with public access

Aalto's Residence and Office (1934–36)
Riihitie 20, Munkkiniemi, Helsinki, Finland
Alvar Aalto Foundation
see below for contact details

Villa Mairea (1937–39)
Ahlström Oy, Noormarkku, Turku, Finland
Tel: +358 (0)10 888 4460
Fax: +358 (0)10 888 4462
Museum of Finnish Architecture
Tel: + 358 (0)9 661 918

Aalto's Summer Residence (1953)
Melalamentie, Muuratsalo, Finland
Järvenpää Town Tourist Services
Tel: +358 (0)9 271 927
Alvar Aalto Foundation
see below for contact details

Aalto's Studio and Office (1955–62)
Tiilimäkizo, Munkkiniemi, Helsinki, Finland
Alvar Aalto Foundation
see below for contact details

Villa Kokkonen (1967–69)
Tuulimyllyntie 5, Järvenpää, Finland
Tel: +358 (0)9 286 204
Jyväskylä Regional Tourist Services
Tel: +358 (0)14 624 903

Public or non-residential buildings

Paimio Sanatorium and Housing Complex (1929–33)
Paimio, Finland
Tel: +358 (0)2 474 5440

Savoy Restaurant (1937)
E. Esplanadikatu 14, 8th floor, Helsinki, Finland
Tel: +358 (0)9 68 44 020

Baker Dormitory, Massachusetts Institute of Technology (1947–48)
362 Mermaid Dr., Cambridge, Massachusetts
Tel: (617) 253 3161

Jyväskylä University (1952–54)
Seminaarinkatu 15, Jyväskylä, Finland
Tel: +358 (0)14 260 1152
Jyväskylä Regional Tourist Services
Tel: +358 (0)14 624 903

Central Finnish Museum (1957–60) and Alvar Aalto Museum (1971–73)
Alvar Aallon katu 7, Jyväskylä, Finland
Tel: +358 (0)14 624 809
Fax: +358 (0)14 619 009
e-mail: museo@alvaraalto.fi

Finlandia Hall (1962–71)
Mannerheimintie 13, Helsinki, Finland
Tel: +358 (0)9 40241
Fax: +358 (0)9 446 259
e-mail: finlandiahall@fin.hel.fi
finlandia.hel.fi

Library, Mount Angel Abbey (1965–70)
Saint Benedict, Oregon
Tel: (503) 845 3303

Kaufman Conference Rooms
809 UN Plaza, Institute of International Education, 12th floor, New York, New York
Tel: (212) 883 8200

Places to stay

Säynätsalo Town Hall Guest Rooms (1950–52)
Parviaisenkatu 9, Säynätsalo, nr Jyväskylä, Finland
Tel: +358 (0)14 623 801
Fax: +358 (0)14 623 802

Books

Quantrill, Malcolm, *Alvar Aalto: A Critical Study*, New Amsterdam Books, 1990.
Reed, Peter et al, *Alvar Aalto: Between Humanism and Materialism*, Museum of Modern Art, 1998.
Schildt, Goran, *Alvar Aalto: The Complete Catalogue of Architecture, Design and Art*, Rizzoli International Publications, 1994.
Schildt, Goran, *Alvar Aalto: Masterworks*, Thames & Hudson, 1998.
Trencher, Michael, *The Alvar Aalto Guide*, Princeton Architectural Press, 1996.
Weston, Richard, *Alvar Aalto*, Phaidon, 1995.

Further information

Alvar Aalto Foundation
Tiilimäki 20, FIN 00330, Helsinki, Finland
Tel: +358 (0)9 4243 3300
Fax: +358 (0)9 485 119
e-mail: foundation@alvaraalto.fi
alvaraalto.fi

Tadao Ando

Houses with public access

There are no houses open to the general public but the following can be viewed from the exterior.

Kidosaki Residence (1982–86)
Setagaya-ku, Tokyo, Japan

Public or non-residential buildings

Church of Light (1988)
Ibaraki, Osaka, Japan

Collezione (1989)
6-1-3 Minami-aoyama, Minato-ku, Harajuku, Tokyo, Japan

Museum of Literature (1989–91)
Himeji, Hyogo, Kansai, Japan

Places to stay

Benesse House/Naoshima Contemporary Art Museum (1992)
Gotanji Naoshimacho, Kagawa-gun, Japan
Tel: +81 8 7892 2030

Books

Blaser, Werner et al, *Tadao Ando: Architecture of Silence*, Birkhauser Verlag, 2001.
Dal Co, Francesco, *Tadao Ando*, Phaidon, 1997.
Fields, D. et al, *Tadao Ando: Dormant Lines*, Rizzoli International Publications, 1991.
Frampton, Kenneth, *Tadao Ando*, Rizzoli International Publications, 1989.
Furuyama, Masao, *Tadao Ando*, Birkhauser Verlag, 1996.
Jodidio, Philip, *Tadao Ando*, Taschen, 1999.
Pare, Richard, *Tadao Ando: The Colours of Light*, Phaidon, 1996.
Zabalbeascoa, Anatxu, *Tadao Ando: Architecture and Spirit*, Gustvo Gili, 1998.

Further information

Tadao Ando Architect & Associates
5-23 Toyosaki 2-Chome Kita-ku, Osaksa 531–0072, Japan
Tel: +81 6 6375 1148
Fax: +81 6 6374 6240

Luis Barragán

Houses with public access

Folke Egerstrom House and San Cristobal Stud Farm (1967–68)
Los Clubes, Mexico City, Mexico

Public or non-residential buildings

Casa-Museo Luis Barragán (1947)
Cerrada General Francisco Ramírez, Tacubaya,
Mexico City, Mexico
Tel: +52 5 272 49 45
Fax: +52 5 515 49 08

Chapel for the Capuchinas Sacramentarias del Purisimo Corazon de Maria (1952–55)
Tlulpan, Mexico

Los Clubes (1964)
Mexico City, Mexico

Gilardi Residence (1975–77)
Tacubaya, Mexico City, Mexico

Books

Burri, Rene, *Luis Barragán,* Phaidon, 2000.
Eggener, Keith L., *Luis Barragán's Gardens of El Pedregal*, Princeton Architectural Press, 2001.
Julbez, Jose Maria Buendia et al, *The Life and Work of Luis Barragán*, Rizzoli International Publications, 1997.
Martinez, Antonio Riggen et al, *Luis Barragán*, Monacelli Press, 1997.
Portugal, Armando Salas, *Luis Barragán*, Rizzoli International Publications, 1993.
Saito, Yutaka, *Luis Barragán*, Noriega Editions, 1995.
Siza, Alvaro, *Barragán: The Complete Works*, Princeton Architectural Press, 1996.
Zanco, Frederico et al, *Luis Barragán: The Quiet Revolution*, Skira Editore, 2000.

Marcel Breuer

Houses with public access

There are no houses open to the public but the New Canaan Historical Society organizes guided tours and the SPNEA organizes walking tours around the Woods End Colony (1939), Massachusetts.

New Canaan Historical Society
13 Oenoke Ridge, New Canaan, Conneticut
Tel: (203) 966 1776
Fax: (203) 972 5017
e-mail: newcanaan.historical@snet.net
nchistory.org

Society for the Preservation of New England Antiquities (SPNEA)
141 Cambridge Street, Boston, Massachusetts
Tel: (617) 227 3956
spnea.org

Public or non-residential buildings

UNESCO headquarters (1958)
7, place de Fontenoy, Paris, France
UNESCO Vistor's Service
Tel: +33 (0)1 45 68 16 42
Fax: +33 (0)1 45 68 56 42

Whitney Museum of American Art (1966)
945 Madison Avenue, New York, New York
Tel: (212) 570 3676
whitney.org

Books

Driller, Joachim, *Breuer Houses*, Phaidon, 2000.
Droste, Magdalena, *Marcel Breuer*, Taschen, 1992.
Gatje, Bob, *Marcel Breuer*, Monacelli Press, 2001.
Masello, *David, Architecture Without Rules: The Houses of Marcel Breuer and Herbert Beckhard*, W. W. Norton & Company, Inc., 1996.
Wilk, Christopher, *Marcel Breuer: Furniture and Interiors*, Architectural Press, 1981.

Connell, Ward, Lucas

Houses with public access

There are no houses open to the general public but the following can be viewed from the exterior.

Kent House (1936)
Ferdinand Street, Chalk Farm, London, England

66 Frognal (1937)
Frognal, Hampstead, London, England

Books

Sharp, Dennis, *Connell Ward Lucas*, Bookart, 1994.

Le Corbusier

Houses with public access

Villa La Lac (1923)
21, route de Lavaux, Corseaux, Swizterland
Tel: +41 21 923 53 63

Villa La Roche (1923)
8–10, square du Docteur Blanche, Paris, France
Fondation Le Corbusier
see below for contact details

Villa Weissenhofsiedlung (1927)
7000 Stuttgart, Germany
Tel: +49 (0)711 85 46 41

Villa Savoye (1928)
82 Chemin de Villiers, Poissy-sur-Seine, France
Tel: +33 (0)1 39 65 01 06

Maisons Jaoul (1951)
83, rue de Longchamp, Neuilly-sur-Seine, France
Tel: +33 (0)1 43 79 66 14

Public or non-residential buildings

Pavillon Suisse (1930)
7, boulevard Jourdan, Paris, France
Tel: +33 (0)3 44 16 10 10

L'Unité d'Habitation (1946–52)
280 boulevard Michelet, Marseille, France
Tel: +33 (0)4 91 16 78 00

Chapelle Notre Dame du Haut (1950–54)
Colline de Bourlémont, Ronchamp, France
Monastery of Sainte Marie de la Tourette,
Departementale 19, Eveux-sur-Arbrere, France
Tel: +33 (0)3 84 20 65 13

Places to stay

Hotel Le Corbusier at L'Unité d'Habitation
280 boulevard Michelet, Marseille, France
Tel: +33 (0)4 91 77 18 15

Further information

Fondation Le Corbusier
Villa La Roche, 8-10, square du Docteur Blanche, 75016 Paris, France
Tel: +33 (0)3 42 88 41 53
Fax: +33 (0)3 42 88 33 17
fondationlecorbusier.asso.fr

Books

Botta, Mario et al, *Le Corbusier*, Princeton
University Press, 1999.

Corbusier, Le, *Essential Le Corbusier: L'Espirit
Nouveau Articles*, Architectural Press, 1998.

Corbusier, Le, *Towards a New Architecture*,
Architectural Press, 1992.

Curtis, William J.R., *Le Corbusier*, Phaidon, 1992.

Frampton, Kenneth, *Le Corbusier*, Thames &
Hudson, 2001.

Gans, Deborah, *The Le Corbusier Guide*,
Princeton Architectural Press, 1998.

Gardiner, Stephen, *Le Corbusier*, Da Capo Press,
1988.

Jenger, Jean et al, *Le Corbusier: Architect,
Painter, Poet*, Harry N. Abrams Inc., 1996.

Jencks, Charles, *Le Corbusier and the
Continental Revolution in Architecture*,
Monacelli Press, 2000.

Stoller, Ezra et al, *The Chapel of Ronchamp*,
Princeton Architectural Press, 1999.

Charles and Ray Eames

Houses with public access

Eames Residence/Case Study House No. 8 (1949)

201 Chautauqua Boulevard, Santa Monica,
California

Eames Office

see below for contact details

Books

Albrecht, Donald et al, *The Work of Charles
and Ray Eames: A Legacy of Invention*,
Harry N. Abrams, 1997.

Drexler, Arthur, *Charles Eames: Furniture from
the Design Collection*, MOMA, New York,
1973.

Kirkham Pat, *Charles and Ray Eames: Designers
of the Century*, MIT Press, 1995.

Neuhart, John et al, *Eames Design*, Harry N.
Abrams, 2000.

Steele, James, *Eames House*, Phaidon, 1994.

Further information

Eames Office Gallery

2665 Main Street, Suite E, Santa Monica,
CA 90405

Tel: (310) 396 5991

eamesoffice.com

Herman Miller, Inc.

855 East Main Avenue, PO Box 302, Zeeland,
MI 49464-0302

Tel: 888 443 4357 (US and Cananda only)

hermanmiller.com

hmeurope.com

*Manufacturers of original Eames furniture,
branches throughout Europe, the US, the Far
East and Middle East*

Walter Gropius

Houses with public access

Directors' Residences (1926–27)

Ebertalle 59–71, Dessau, Germany

Visitors' Services

Tel: +49 (0)340 6508 251

Fax: +49 (0)340 6508 226

e-mail: besuch@bauhaus-dessau.de

bauhaus-dessau.de

Weissenhofsiedlung (1927)

7000 Stuttgart, Germany

Tel: +49 (0)711 85 46 41

Gropius Residence (1938)

68 Baker Bridge Road, Lincoln, Massachusetts

SPNEA

Tel: (617) 227 3956

spnea.org

Public or non-residential buildings

Fagus Factory (1911–13)

Alfred an der Leine, Germany

Walter Gropius with Maxwell Fry

Bauhaus Building (1919–25)

Gropiusallee 38, Dessau, Germany

Visitors' Services

Tel: +49 (0)340 6508 251

Fax: +49 (0)340 6508 226

e-mail: besuch@bauhaus-dessau.de

bauhaus-dessau.de

Impington Village College (1936–40)

New Road, Impington, Cambridgeshire, England

Tel: +44 (0)1223 200400

Fax: +44 (0)1223 200419

impington.cambs.sch.uk

Pan Am Building (1963)

200 Park Avenue at 43rd Street, New York,
New York

Tel: (212) 922 9100

*This is now known as the MetLife building
after being sold by Pan Am in 1981.*

Harvard Graduate Center

Cambridge, Massachusetts

harvard.edu

Books

Berdini, Paolo, *Walter Gropius*, Gustavo Gili, 1994.

Gideon, S., *Walter Gropius: Work and
Teamwork*, Architectural Press, 1954.

Gropius, Walter, *The New Architecture and
the Bauhaus*, MIT Press, 1965.

Nerdinger, Winfried et al, *The Walter Gropius
Archive*, Garland Publishing, Inc., 1990.

Oliver Hill

Houses with public access

There are no houses open to the general
public but the 20th Century Society organizes
guided tours around the Frinton Park Estate
(1934–37), Frinton-on-Sea, Essex, England.

Public or non-residential buildings

Midland Hotel (1933)

Morecombe, Lancashire, England

Friends of the Midland Hotel

Tel: +44 (0)1524 34189

e-mail: friends@midlandhotel.org

midlandhotel.org

Prospect Inn

Minster in Thanet, Kent, England

Books

Powers, Alan, *Oliver Hill: Architect, Lover of
Life*, Mouton Publications, 1989.

Arne Jacobsen

Houses with public access

There are no houses open to the general
public.

Public or non-residential buildings

Saint Catherine's College (1959–60)
Manor Road, Oxford, England
General Office
Tel: +44 (0)1865 271701
Fax: +44 (0)1865 271768

Munkegard School (1952–56)
Vangedevej 178, Soburg, Copenhagen,
Denmark

Places to stay

Radisson S.A.S. Royal Hotel Copenhagen (1956–60)
Hammerichgade 1–5, Copenhagen, Denmark
Tel: +45 33 42 60 00
Fax: +45 33 42 61 00
Reservations: +33 42 62 00
e-mail: cphzh@cphza.rdsas.com
radisson.com
The hotel has recently undergone refurbishent but room 606 has been preserved exactly to Jacobsen's original design

Books

Arne Jacobsen, Stedelijk Museum,1959.
Solaguren-Beascoa, Felix, *Arne Jacobsen*,
    Rizzoli International Publications, 1991.
Than, Thorsten and Vindum Kjeid, *Arne
    Jacobsen*, Arkitektens Forlag, 1998

Pierre Koenig

Houses with public access

There are no houses open to the general public but the Society of Architectural Historians (see above for contact details) organize guided tours.

Books

Steel, J. and Jenkins, D., *Pierre Koenig*,
    Phaidon, 1998.

Further information

Pierre Koenig Archives
e-mail: pfkoenig@mizar.usc.edu
rcf.usc.edu/~pfkoenig
usc.edu/dept/architecture/slide/koenig

John Lautner

Houses with public access

There are no houses open to the general public but various societies organize guided tours and the following can be viewed from the exterior.

Lautner Residence (1939)
2007 Micheltorena, Los Angeles, California

Sheats-Goldstein Residence (1948)
10901 Strathmore, Beverly Hills,
California
This house was used as a location in the movie The Big Lebowski *(Ethan and Joel Coen, 1998)*

Malin Residence (Chemosphere) (1960)
776 Torreyson Drive, Los Angeles, California
This house is now known as the Kuhn Residence and was used as a location in the movies Body Double *(Brian de Palma, 1984)* and Charlie's Angels *(Joseph Nichols, 2000)*

Elrod Residence (1968)
2175 Southridge Drive, Palm Springs,
California
This house was used as a location in the movie Diamonds are Forever *(Guy Hamilton, 1971)*

Reiner-Burchill Residence (Silvertop) (1963)
2138 Micheltorena, Los Angeles, California
This house was used as a location in the movie Less Than Zero *(Marek Kanievska, 1987)*

Books

Campbell-Lange, Barbara-Ann, *John Launter*,
    Taschen, 1999.
Escher, Frank C. (ed), *John Launter: Architect*,
    Artemis, 1994.
Hess, Alan, *The Architecture of John Launter*,
    Rizzoli International Publications, 1999.

Further information

The John Lautner Foundation
PO Box 29517, Los Angeles,
CA 90029
Tel: (323) 951 1061
Fax: (213) 413 7058
e-mail: lautner@johnlautner.org
johnlautner.org

Richard Meier

Houses with public access

There are no houses open to the general public.

Public or non-residential buildings

The Atheneum (1975–79)
Historic New Harmony, University of Southern Indiana, PO Box 579, New Harmony, Indiana
Tel: (812) 682 4474
Tel: (812) 682 4488
e-mail: harmony@usi.edu
newharmony.org

Sarah Campbell Blaffer Pottery Studio (1975–78)
Historic New Harmony
see above for contact details

The Aye Simon Reading Room (1977–78)
Solomon R. Guggenheim Museum,
1071 5th Avenue, New York, New York
Tel: (212) 423 3500
guggenheim.org

Books

Jodidio, Philip, *Richard Meier*, Taschen, 1995.
Meier, Richard, *Richard Meier Architect Vol. 1*,
    Rizzoli International Publications, 1984.
Meier, Richard, *Richard Meier Architect Vol. 2*,
    Rizzoli International Publications, 1991.
Meier, Richard, *Richard Meier Houses*, Rizzoli
    International Publications, 1996.
Meier, Richard, *Richard Meier in Europe*, Ernst &
    Sohn, 1996.
Meier, Richard, *The Ackerberg House and
    Addition*, Monacelli Press, 1996.

Further information

Richard Meier & Partners
475 10th Avenue, New York, NY 10018
Tel: (212) 967 6060
richardmeier.com

George Nelson

Houses with public access

There are no houses open to the general public.

Books

Abercrombie, Stanley, *George Nelson: The Design of Modern Design*, MIT Press, 1994.

Further information

Herman Miller, Inc.
855 East Main Avenue, PO Box 302, Zeeland, MI 49464-0302
Tel: 888 443 4357 (US and Cananda only)
hermanmiller.com
hmeurope.com
Manufacturers of original Nelson furniture, branches throughout Europe, the US, the Far East and Middle East

Vitra Design Museum
see above for contact details
The Vitra Design Museum holds the George Nelson Archive

Richard Neutra

Houses with public access

VDL House and Neutra Colony (1933)
2300 Silverlake Boulevard, Silverlake, California
California Polytechnic University, Pomona
e-mail: jnstone@earthlink.net
This house was destroyed by fire in 1963 but was rebuilt by Richard Neutra's son, Dion, the following year

The Society of Architectural Historians (see above for contact details) organize guided tours to a number of other Neutra houses.

Books

Hines, Thomas, *Richard Neutra and Modern Architecture*, University of California Press, 1994.
Lamprecht, Barbara, *Richard Neutra: Complete Works*, Taschen, 2000.
Leet, Stephen, *Richard Neutra's Miller House*, Princeton Architectural Press, 2001.
McCoy, Esther, *Richard Neutra*, George Braziller, Inc., 2001.
Neutra, Dione, *Richard Neutra: Promise and Fulfillment, 1919–1932*, Southern Illinois University Press, 2000.
Sack, Manfred, *Richard Neutra*, Ellipsis, 1992.

Further information

Dion Neutra
Institute for Survival Through Design
2440 Neutra Place, Los Angeles, CA 90039
Tel: (323) 666 1806
e-mail: dionn@aol.com
neutra.org

Verner Panton

Books

Panton, Verner, *Verner Panton: The Complete Works*, Vitra Design Museum, 1986.

Further information

vernerpanton.com

Gio Ponti

Houses with public access

There are no houses open to the general public.

Public or non-residential buildings

Pirelli Tower (1956)
Piazza Duca d'Aousta 5, Milan, Italy

Places to stay

Hotel Parco dei Principi
Vita Rota 1, Sorrento 80067, Italy
Tel: +39 (0)81 878 4588
Fax: +39 (0)81 878 3786
grandhotelparcodeiprincipi.it

Books

Enzo, Frateli et al, *Gio Ponti*, Rizzoli International Publications, 1996.
Gio Ponti, Salone Internazionale del Mobile, 1997.

Further information

Galleria Neoponti
7–9 North Dean Street, Englewood, NJ 07631
gioponti.com

Ludwig Mies van der Rohe

Houses with public access

Haus Lange and Haus Esters (1928)
Wilhelmshofallee 91 & 97, Krefeld, Germany
Museum Haus Lange and Museum Haus Esters
Tel: +49 (0)2151 77 00 44
krefeld.de

Farnsworth Residence (1946–51)
14520 River Road, Plano, Illinois
Chicago Architecture Foundation (CAF)
see above for contact details

Lake Shore Drive Apartments (1951)
860–880 Lake Shore Drive, Chicago, Illinois
Chicago Architecture Foundation (CAF)
see above for contact details

Public or non-residential buildings

German Pavilion (1929)
Avda. del Marquès de Comillas, s/n, Montjuïc, Barcelona, Spain
Tel: +34 934 23 40 16
Fax: +34 934 26 37 72
e-mail: pavello@miesbcn.com

Seagram Building (1957)
375 Park Avenue, New York, New York

Neue Nationalgalerie (1965–68)
Potsdamerstrasse 50, Tiergarten, Berlin, Germany
Tel: +49 (0)30 266 26 62
smb.spk-berlin.de

Books

Blaser, Werner, *Mies van der Rohe*, Birkhäuser Verlag, 1997.
Blaser, Werner, *Mies van der Rohe: Lake Shore Drive Apartments*, Birkhäuser Verlag, 1999.
Carter, Peter, *Mies van der Rohe at Work*, Phaidon, 1999.
Detlef, Martins (ed), *The Presence of Mies*, Princeton Architectural Press, 1994.
Ludwig Mies van der Rohe, Museum of Modern Art, 1977.
Safran, Yehuda E., *Mies van der Rohe*, Gustavo Gili, 2001.
Tegethoff, Wolf et al, *Ludwig Mies van der Rohe: Tugendhat House*, Springer, 1998.

Further information

Fundació Mies van der Rohe
Provença 318, pral. 2B 08037, Barcelona, Spain
Tel: +34 932 15 10 11
Fax: +34 934 88 36 85
e-mail: miesbcn@miesbcn.com
miesbcn.com

Paul Rudolph and the Sarasota School

Houses with public access

There are no houses open to the general public but the Sarsota Fine Art Society (e-mail: leibgal@aol.com) organize guided tours.

Public or non-residential buildings

Sarasota High School (Paul Rudolph, 1958)
Sarasota, Florida

Yale Art and Architecture Building (Paul Rudolph , 1961–63)
New Haven, Connecticut

Places to stay

Warm Mineral Springs (Victor Lundy, 1960)
12597 South Tamiami Trail, Venice, Florida
Tel: (941) 426 4029

Books

Howey, John, *The Sarasota School of Architecture*, MIT Press, 1995.
Moholy-Nagy, Sibyl and Scwab, Gerhard, *The Architecture of Paul Rudolph*, Praeger 1970.
'On Parallell Lines: The Sarasota Modern Movement and The Case Study House Program', Society of Architectural Historians/ Southern California Chapter, January 2001.

Rudolph Schindler

Houses with public access

Schindler Residence and Studio (1922)
833 North Kings Road, West Hollywood, California
MAK Center for Art and Architecture
see below for contact details

Mackey Apartments (1939)
1137–41 South Cochran Avenue, Los Angeles, California
MAK Center for Art and Architecture
see below for contact details

Public or non-residential buildings

Sardis Restaurant
6313 Hollywood Boulevard, Hollywood, California

Books

The Architecture of R. M. Schindler, Musuem of Contemporary Art, Los Angeles, 2001.
Noever, Peter et al, *Rudolf M. Schindler*, MAK Center for Art and Architecture, 2000.
Sheine, Judith, *R. M. Schindler: Works and Projects*, Gustavo Gili, 1998.
Smith, Kathryn, *Schindler House*, Harry N. Abrams, 2001.
Steele, James, *R. M. Schindler*, Taschen, 1999.

Further information

MAK Center for Art and Architecture
835 North Kings Road, West Hollywood, CA 90069-5409
Tel: (323) 651 1510
Fax: (323) 651 2340
e-mail: MAKcenter@earthlink.net
makcenter.com

Harry Seidler

Houses with public access

Rose Seidler Residence (1948–50)
71 Clissold Road, Wahroonga, Sydney, N.S.W., Australia
Tel: +61 (0)2 9989 8020
Fax: +61 (0)2 9487 2761
hht.nsw.gov.au

Public or non-residential buildings

Harry Seidler Offices and Apartments (1970)
2 Glen Street, Milsons Point, Sydney, N.S.W., Australia

Waverley City Council (1982–84)
293 Springvale Road, Waverly, Victoria, Australia

Waverley Art Gallery (1990)
170 Jells Road, Wheelers Hill, Waverley, Victoria, Australia

Places to stay

Hilton Hotel (1983–86)
190 Elizabeth Street, Brisbane, Queensland, Australia
Tel: +61 (0)7 3234 2000
hilton.com

Books

Frampton, K. and Drew, P., *Harry Seidler: Four Decades of Architecture*, Thames & Hudson, 1992.

Further information

Harry Seidler & Associates
Level 5, 2 Glen Street, Milsons Point, Sydney, N.S.W., Australia
Tel: +61 (0)2 9922 1388
Fax: +61 (0)2 9957 2947
e-mail: hsa@seidler.net.au
seidler.net.au

Wells Coates

Houses with public access

There are no houses open to the general public but the following can be viewed from the exterior.

Lawn Road Flats (1933)
Lawn Road, Hampstead, London, England
Isokon Trust
e-mail: pfarch@aol.com
Notting Hill Housing Group
Tel: +44 (0)20 8357 5000
Fax: +44 (0)20 8357 5299
nhhg.org.uk

Embassy Court (1934–35)
Kings Road, Brighton, East Sussex, England

Books

Cohn, Laura, *Door to a Secret Room: A Portrait of Wells Coates*, Ashgate Publishing Company, 1999.
Fraser, Gordon, *Wells Coates*, Sherban Cantarzino, 1978.

Wells Coates and Patrick Gwynne

Houses with public access

The Homewood (1938)
Portsmouth Road, Esher, Surrey, England
The National Trust
Tel: +44 (0)1372 467 806
Fax: +44 (0)1372 464 394
e-mail: sclgen@smtp.ntrust.org.uk
nationaltrust.org.uk

Frank Lloyd Wright

Houses with public access

Robie Residence (1909)
5757 Woodlawn Avenue, Chicago, Illinois
University of Chicago
Tel: (312) 702 8374

Hollyhock House (1921)
Barsndall Art Park, 4808 Hollywood Boulevard,
Los Angeles, California
Tel: (213) 485 4851
*This house is currently being renovated but is
due to reopen in 2003*

Ennis-Brown House (1924)
2655 Glendower Avenue, Los Angeles,
California
Trust for Preservation of Cultural Heritage
Tel: (213) 660 0607
ennisbrownhouse.org
*This house been used as a location for many
movies including* Blade Runner *(Ridley Scott,
1982),* Black Rain *(Ridley Scott, 1988), and*
Grand Canyon *(Lawrence Kasdan, 1991).*

Fallingwater (1936)
Route 381, Bear Run, Pennsylvania
Western Pennsylvanian Conservancy
Tel: (412) 329 8501

Public or non-residential buildings

Taliesin (1911-38)
Route 23, Spring Green, Wisconsin, Illinois
Frank Lloyd Wright Foundation
see below for contact details

Florida Southern College (1938-54)
111 Lake Hollingworth Drive, Lakeland,
Florida
Tel: (863) 680 4110

Solomon R Guggenheim Museum (1956)
5th Avenue, New York, New York
Tour and Group Services
Tel: (212) 423 3555

Places to stay

Baron Island (1950)
Murcia, Spain
Elysian Holidays
16a High Street, Tenterden, Kent TN30 6AP,
England
Tel: +44 (0)1580 766599
Fax: +44 (0)1580 765416
e-mail: holidays@elysianholidays.co.uk
elysian holidays.co.uk

Books

Gebhard, David et al, *The California
Architecture of Frank Lloyd Wright*,
Chronicle Books, 1997.

Heinz, Thomas A., *Frank Lloyd Wright:
Interiors and Furniture*, Academy Editions,
1994.

Kaufmann, Edgar J., *Fallingwater*, Abbeville
Press, 1993.

Larkin, David and Pfeiffer, Bruce Brooks, *Frank
Lloyd Wright: Master Builder*, Thames &
Hudson, 1997.

Larkin, David and Pfeiffer, Bruce Brooks, *Frank
Lloyd Wright: The Masterworks*, Rizzoli
International Publications, 1993.

Legler, Dixie, *Frank Lloyd Wright: The Western
Work*, Chronicle Books, 1999.

Levine, Neil, *The Architecture of Frank Lloyd
Wright*, Princeton Architectural Press, 1995.

McCarter, Robert et al, *Frank Lloyd Wright:
Architect*, Phaidon, 1999.

Riley, Terence et al, *Frank Lloyd Wright*,
Museum of Modern Art, 1994.

Stoller, Ezra, *Frank Lloyd Wright's
Fallingwater*, Princeton Architectural Press,
1999.

Thomson, Iain, *Frank Lloyd Wright: A Visual
Encyclopedia*, Thunder Bay Press, 2000.

Waggoner, Lynda S. and Western Pennsylvania
Conservancy, *Fallingwater: Frank Lloyd
Wright's Romance with Nature*, Rizzoli
International Publications, 1996.

Wright, Frank Lloyd, *Modern Architecture*,
South Illinois University Press, 1987.

Further information

Frank Lloyd Wright Foundation
Taliesin, 5481 County Highway, Spring Green,
WI 53588
Tel: (608) 588 2511
Fax: (608) 588 2090
e-mail: flwfdn@franklloydwrightorg
Taliesin West, PO Box 4430, Scottsdale,
AZ 85261-4430
Tel: (480) 860 2700
Fax: (480) 391 4009
e-mail: flwfdn@franklloydwrightorg
franklloydwright.org

Frank Lloyd Wright Preservation Trust
951 Chicago Avenue, Oak Park, IL 60302
Tel: (708) 848 1976
Fax: (708) 848 1248
e-mail: flwpr@wrightplus.org
wrightplus.org

The Wright Web Guide
cypgrp.com/flw

SUPPLIERS

Brick

Brick Industry Association (BIA)
11490 Commerce Park Drive, Reston, VA 28191-1525
Tel: (703) 620 0010
Fax: (703) 620 3928
e-mail: brickinfo@bia.org
brickinfo.org
General information on bricks. List of manufacturers and distributors throughout the US

Glen-Gery Brick
PO Box 7001, 1166 Spring Street, Wyomissing, PA 19610-6001
Tel: (610) 374 4011
Fax: (610) 374 1622
glengerybrick.com
Wide range of facing bricks and brick pavoirs available. List of distributors throughout the US

Pacific Clay Products
14741 Lake Street, Lake Elsinore, CA 92530-1609
Tel: (909) 674 2131
Fax: (909) 674 4909
e-mail: info@pacificclay.com
pacificclay.com
Wide range of facing bricks and brick pavoirs available. List of distributors throughout the US

Concrete

American Concrete Institute International
PO Box 9094, Farmington Hills, MI 48333
Tel: (248) 848 3700
e-mail: webmaster@aci-int.org
aci-int.org
General information on concrete. List of manufacturers and distributors throughout the US

A to Z Precast Concrete Products, Inc.
4451 8th Avenue South, St Petersburg, FL 33711
Tel: (800) 345 7821
Fax: (727) 328 2234
e-mail: sales@atozprecast.com
atozprecast.com
Wide range of concrete products available including precast concrete decking, fencing and custom-designed building elements

Operative Plasterers' and Cement Masons International Association (OP&CMIA)
14405 Laurel Place, Suite 300, Laurel, ML 20708
Tel: (301) 470 4200
Fax: (301) 470 2502
e-mail: opcmiaintl@opcmia.org
opcmia.org
General information on concrete. List of recommended cement masons throughout the US

Stone paving and gravel

LB Stone, Inc.
PO Box 276, 167 Maple Street, Apple Creek, OH 44606
Tel: (330) 698 3931
Fax: (330) 698 4432
e-mail: lbstone167@aol.com
lb-stone.com
Wide range of stone products available including paving tiles, veneers, and slate flooring

Resource Building Products
Stanton Store, 10961 Dale Street, Stanton, CA 90860
Tel: (714) 952 2993
Fax: (714) 952 2710
e-mail: info@bricknstone.com
bricknstone.com
Wide range of stone flooring and decorative gravel available

Scott System, Inc.
1788 Helena Street, Aurora, CO 80011
Tel: (303) 341 1400
Fax: (714) 341 1995
e-mail: info@scottsystem.com
scottsystem.com
Wide range of textured concrete in standard patterns or custom-designed available

Stone Network
e-mail: info@stone-network.com
stone-network.com
General information on stone. List of manufacturers and distributors of natural stone products including granite, marble, limestone, sandstone, and slate throughout the US

Tilt-up Concrete Association
PO Box 204, Mount Vernon, IA 52314
Tel: (319) 895 6911
Fax: (319) 895 8830
e-mail: esauter@tilt-up.org
tilt-up.org
General information on conrete. List of suppliers throughout the US

Timber, cladding, and decking

Archadeck
2112 West Laburnum Avenue, Suite 100, Richmond, VA 23227
Tel: (800) 722 4668
archadeck.com
Range of pre-built and custom-designed decking available

Decks USA
PO Box 6217, Youngstown, OH 44501-6217
Tel: (330) 788 7882
e-mail: contact@decksusa.com
decksusa.com
Range of pre-built and custom-designed decking available

Friends of the Earth
1025 Vermont Avenue, NW Washington, DC 20005
Tel: (202) 783 7400
Fax: (202) 783 0444
e-mail: foe@foe.org
foe.org
General information on eco-friendly timber products. List of suppliers of hardwoods from sustainable sources throughout the US

John Cox Lumber Company
PO Box 9504, 202 73rd Street, Houston, TX 77261
Tel: (713) 921 4163
Fax: (713) 921 0962
e-mail: info@coxhardware.com
coxhardware.com
Wide range of timber products from sustainable sources available. List of distributors throughout the US

Windows and doors

Dawson Metal Company, Inc.
825 Allen Street, PO Box 0278, Jamestown, NJ 14701
Tel: (716) 664 3811
Fax: (716) 661 3722
e-mail: dawson@dawsondoors.com
dawsonmetal.com
Wide range of steel-framed windows and doors available

Winstrom Manufacturing
70 North Street, Park Forest, IL 60466
Tel: (708) 748 8200
Fax: (708) 748 8222
e-mail: sales@winstromwindows.com
winstromwindows.com
Wide range of speciality and architectural windows available including aluminum-framed windows

Timber flooring

Authentic Pine Floors, Inc.
4042 Highway, 42 Locust Grove, GA 30248
Tel: (770) 957 6038
Fax: (770) 914 2925
e-mail: sharon@authenticpinefloors.com
authenticpinefloors.com
Wide range of pine flooring available including new and reclaimed timber

National Wood Flooring Association (NWFA)
16388 Westwoods Business Park, Ellisville, MO 63021
Tel (US): (800) 422 4556
Tel (Can): (800) 848 8824
Fax: (636) 391 5161
e-mail: info@nwfa.org
nwfa.org
woodfloors.org
General information on timber. List of manufacturers and suppliers throughout the US

Tile flooring

Paris Ceramics
150 East 58th Street, 7th floor, New York, NY 10155
Tel: (212) 644 2782
Fax: (212) 644 2875
parisceramics.com
Wide range of new and reclaimed tile flooring available including limestone and mosaic

Walker Zanger
101 Henry Adams Street, Suite 412, San Francisco, CA 94103
Tel: (415) 487 2130
Fax: (415) 487 2135
or
4701 Cameron Street, Suite P, Las Vegas, NV 89103
Tel: (702) 248 1550
Fax: (702) 248 1556
or

7055 Old Katy Road, Houston,
TX 77024
Tel: (713) 880 9292
Fax: (713) 880 8229
or
11550 Newberry, Suite 300,
Dallas, TX 75229
Tel: (972) 481 3900
Fax: (972) 488 3782
walkerzanger.com
*Wide range of tile flooring
available including ceramic,
stone, and mosaic. List of
additional stores throughout
California*

Other floorcoverings

ABC Carpet and Home
881 Broadway, New York,
NY 10003
Tel: (212) 473 3000
or
777 South Congress, Delray
Beach, FL 33445
Tel: (561) 279 7777
abchome.com
*Range of natural floorcoverings
available including coir, jute,
and sisal*

Carousel Carpet Mills, Inc.
1 Carousel Lane, Ukia,
CA 95482
Tel: (707) 485 0333
Fax: (707) 485 5911
*Range of natural
floorcoverings available
including seagrass matting*

Paints

Keim Mineral Systems
Cohalan Company, 62 Port
Lewes, Lewes, DE 19958
Tel: (302) 344 9094
Tel: (302) 644 1007
e-mail:
info@keimmineralsystems.com
keimmineralsystems.com
*Range of long-life, color-fast
masonry paints available with
technical and color consultation*

National Paint and Coatings Association (NPCA)
1500 Rhode Island Avenue,
NW Washington, DC 20005
Tel: (202) 462 6272
Fax: (202) 462 8549
e-mail: npca@paint.org
paint.org
*General information on paint.
List of manufacturers and
suppliers throughout the US*

Painting and Wallcovering Contractor (PWC)
107 West Pacific Avenue,
St Louis, MO 63119-3776
Tel: (314) 961 6644
Fax: (314) 961 4809
e-mail: keberson@finan.com
paintstore.com
*General information on paint.
List of manufacturers and
suppliers throughout the US*

Mural painters

Century
68 Marylebone High Street,
London W1U 5JH, England
Tel: +44 (0)20 7487 5100
Fax: +44 (0)20 7487 5168
e-mail:
shop@centurydesign.f9.co.uk
centuryd.com
understandingmodern.com
*List of recommended local
mural painters throughout
the US*

Swimming pools and water features

Direct Swimming Pool Products
5322 Rafe Banks Drive, Unit D,
Flowery Branch, GA 30542
Tel: (678) 513 9610
e-mail:
sales@swimmingpools.com
swimmingpools.com
*Wide range of pre-built and
custom-designed swimming
pools and spas, accessories, and
associated products*

Waterlines, Inc.
North Church Technical Center,
4 Park Drive, Franklin, NJ 07416
Tel: (973) 209 7777
Fax: (973) 209 7421
e-mail: waterlines@nac.net
waterlinesinc.com
*Wide range of pre-built and
custom-designed swimming
pools and spas, acessories, and
associated products*

Furniture and lighting

Century
68 Marylebone High Street,
London W1U 5JH, England
Tel: +44 (0)20 7487 5100
Fax: +44 (0)20 7487 5168
e-mail:
shop@centurydesign.f9.co.uk
centuryd.com
understandingmodern.com
*Vintage furniture, lighting, and
accessories dating from 1950s
onwards, re-edition furniture,
and contemporary designs.
Designers stocked include
Charles Eames, George Nelson,
and Karim Rashid*

Full Upright Position (FUP)
1200 NW Everett, Portland,
OR 97209
Tel: (800) 431 5134
fup.com
*Re-edition furniture. Designers
stocked include Alvar Aalto,
Marcel Breuer, Charles Eames,
Le Corbusier, and Neils Bendtsen*

International Contract Furnishings, Inc. (ICF Group)
Helikon Showroom,
138 West 25th Street,
New York, NY 10001
Tel: (212) 924 4720
Fax: (212) 924 4875
or
Helikon Showroom,
550 Pacific Avenue,
San Francisco, CA 94133
Tel: (415) 433 3231
Fax: (415) 433 6101

e-mail: info@icfgroup.com
icfgroup.com
*Re-edition furniture. Designers
stocked include Alvar Aalto and
Richard Neutra*

Krypton
707 Monroe Way, Placentia,
CA 92870
Tel: (714) 577 0219
e-mail: modern@krypton1.com
krypton1.com
*Contemporary designs
including furniture, accessories,
and lighting*

Modernica
57 Greene Street, New York,
NY 10012
Tel: (212) 219 1303
e-mail:
nyshowroom@modernica.net
or
555 North Franklin Street,
Chicago, IL 60610
Tel: (312) 222 1808
e-mail:
chshowroom@modernica.net
or
7366 Beverly Boulevard,
Los Angeles, CA 9003
Tel: (323) 933 0383
e-mail:
lashowroom@modernica.net
modernica.net
*Re-edition furniture and
acessories, including bubble
lamps, and contemporary
designs. Designers stocked
include George Nelson*

R Twentieth-century Design
82 Franklin Street, New York,
NY 10013
Tel: (212) 343 7979
e-mail: r@r20thcentury.com
r20thcentury.com
*Contemporary designs
including furniture, accessories,
and lighting*

Senzatempo
1655 Meridian Avenue,
Miami Beach, FL 33139
Tel: (305) 534 5588

Fax: (305) 534 4545
e-mail: style@senzatempo.com
senzatempo.com
*Vintage furniture – designers
stocked include Charles Eames,
Arne Jacobsen and Gio Ponti*

Swank
45 East 7th Street, New York,
NY 1003
Tel: (212) 673 8597
e-mail: decor@swank-nyc.com
*Vintage furniture, accessories,
and lighting. Designers stocked
include Alvar Aalto, Charles
Eames and Knoll*

Vitra
149 5th Avenue, New York,
NY 10010
Tel: (212) 539 1900
Fax: (212) 539 1977
e-mail: info_us@vitra.com
vitra.com
*Re-edition furniture and
contemporary designs,
accessories, and lighting*

ARCHITECTS CONTEMPORARY ARCHITECTS FEATURED IN MODERN NOW

OCEAN RETREAT (PP. 120–23)

Nik Karalis

Woods Bagot

Level 10, 1 Spring Street, Melbourne,

Victoria 3000, Australia

Tel: +613 9650 6610

Fax: +613 9650 6602

e-mail: wbmel@woodsbagot.com.au

MODERNIST REINTERPRETATION (PP. 124–29)

Mark Guard

Mark Guard Associates

161 Whitfield Street, London W1P 5RY,

England

Tel: +44 20 7380 1199

Fax: +44 20 7387 5441

e-mail: info@markguard.com

markguard.com

MINIMALIST VIEWING PLATFORM (PP. 130–33)

John Barman and Kelly Graham

John Barman, Inc.

500 Park Avenue, New York, NY 10022

Tel: (212) 838 9443

Fax: (212) 838 4028

e-mail: info@johnbarman.com

johnbarman.com

BLURRING THE BOUNDARIES (PP. 134–41)

MODERNIST IN INSPIRATION (PP. 150–53)

Kathryn Ogawa and Gilles Depardon

Ogawa/Depardon Architects

137 Varick Street, New York, NY 10013

Tel: (212) 627 7390

Fax: (212) 627 9681

e-mail: ogawdep@aol.com

oga-ny.com

MODERN YET CONTEMPORARY (PP. 146–49)

Mårten Claesson, Eero Koivisto and

Ola Rune

Claesson Koivisto Rune

Sankt Paulsgatan 25, SE–118 48 Stockholm,

Sweden

Tel: +46 (8) 644 58 63

Fax: +46 (8) 644 58 83

e-mail: arkitektkontor@claesson-koivisto-rune.se

scandiandesign.com/claesson-koivisto-

rune

RELAXED OPEN-PLAN SPACE (PP. 154–57)

William Fisher

Marshall Fisher Architects

608–318 Homer Street, Vancouver, Canada

Tel: (604) 681 5741

Fax: (604) 682 7939

e-mail: marshall_fisher@telus.net

OPENING UP THE HOUSE (PP. 158–63)

Andrew Weaving

Century

68 Marylebone High Street, London W1U

5JH, England

Tel: +44 20 7487 5100

Fax: +44 20 7487 5168

e-mail: shop@centurydesign.f9.co.uk

centuryd.com

understandingmodern.com

REINVENTED SPACE (PP. 164–65)

Sager Wimer Coombe Architects

1002–480 Canal Street, New York, NY 10013

Tel: (212) 226 9600

Fax: (212) 226 8456

e-mail: swcarch@aol.com

EVER-SHIFTING COLLAGE (PP. 166–71)

Karim Rashid

Karim Rashid, Inc.

357 West 17th Street, New York, NY 10011

Tel: (212) 929 8657

Fax: (212) 929 0247

e-mail: karim@karimrashid.com

karimrashid.com

180-DEGREE OUTLOOK (PP. 172–73)

Frank Escher and Ravi GuneWardena

Escher GuneWardena Architects

2404 Wilshire Boulevard, Los Angeles,

CA 90057

Tel: (213) 413 2325

Fax: (213) 413 7058

e-mail: egarch@aol.com

egarchitecture.com

1950s... FLAMBOYANTLY RESTYLED (PP. 174–79)

Michael Czysz

Architropolis

10200 SE Cambridge Lane, Portland,

OR 97222

Tel: (503) 786 9007

Fax: (503) 786 5100

architropolis.com

INDEX

AUTHOR'S ACKNOWLEDGMENTS

First of all I should thank Jane O'Shea for passing on my initial ideas for this book to Anne Furniss. It all started there. Thanks to all the architects and designers who have allowed us to photograph and include their work in this book. Special thanks to Frank Escher and Ravi GuneWardena for their introduction to the owners and occupiers of the Lautner houses included, for giving up so much of their time, and driving me around Los Angeles to see some of the best houses in town (unfortunately not all used in this book, but they will crop up somewhere soon, I hope). Thanks to Gilles Depardon for driving me out to Pound Ridge and for building such a great house there. Thanks to all the owners of the homes featured—Douglas and Olivia Walstrom, M.T. Rainey, Karim Rashid, David Zander, Eli Bonerz, Neils and Nancy Bendtsen, and all the others. Thanks for their time, patience and, in some cases, a great lunch. Thanks to Lisa Freedman who had the lengthy task of writing all the text, calling around the world to try to speak to everyone involved, and for getting all the right stuff down on paper. Thanks to Mary Davies for her daily, and sometimes hourly, e-mails or phone calls, which I am now lost without—she opened my eyes to things I take for granted and made MODERN so much easier to UNDERSTAND. Thanks to Andrew Wood, Graham Atkins Hughes, and Martin Tessler for putting up with me and for taking great photos. And, of course, thanks to Helen Lewis who has been involved right from the start and has had the lovely job of putting the whole thing together—she has really understood it all right from the word go. Thanks to Oliver Childs for running the shop while I have been away and, last but not least, thanks to Ian for putting up with my ups and downs while working on this book, and for being there when I needed some moral support.

PUBLISHER'S ACKNOWLEDGMENTS

The publisher has made every effort to trace the copyright holders, architects, and designers featured in this book. We apologize in advance for any unintentional omission and would be pleased to insert the appropriate acknowledgment in any subsequent edition.

1 left Paul Rocheleau; 1 right Michael Moran; 2 Photo © Lluís Casals; 3 Graham Atkins Hughes; 4 Tim Street-Porter; 5 Martin Tessler; 6 Strüwing Reklamefoto; 7 Martin Tessler; 8 Graham Atkins Hughes; 9 Andrew Weaving; 10–11 Graham Atkins Hughes; 12–13 ESTO/Ezra Stoller; 14–15 Paul Rocheleau; 16 left Robert Sweeney/Friends of the Schindler House, gift of Mrs Richard Schindler; 16 right Michael Freeman; 17 Julius Shulman; 18 Isokon Plus Archive; 19 above Bauhaus-Archiv Berlin; 19 below Bauhaus-Archiv Berlin/foto: Lucia Moholy; 20 Lucien Hervé, Paris/©FLC/ADAGP, Paris; 21 Herbert Ypma; 22 Paul Rocheleau; 23 Hedrich Blessing; 24 British Architectural Library, RIBA, London; 25 above Edifice/Larraine Worpole; 25 below British Architectural Library, RIBA, London; 26 Paul Rocheleau; 27 Vitra Design Museum, Weil am Rhein; 28 above © Lucia Eames/Eames office (eamesoffice.com); 28 below © Lucia Eames/Eames Office (eamesoffice.com)/David Travers; 29 Julius Shulman; 30 left Alvar Aalto Archives, Helsinki; 30 right Polfoto/Erik Gleie; 31 above Undine Pröhl; 31 below Gio Ponti Photo Archives/Domus magazine, 1948; 32 Marirosa Toscani Ballo; 33 above Julius Shulman; 33 below Vitra Design Museum, Weil am Rhein/Verner Panton Design; 34 ESTO/Scott Frances; 35 Mitsuo Matsuoka/Tadao Ando Architect & Associates; 36–39 Graham Atkins Hughes; 40 Agence Top/Robert Cesar; 41 above Agence Top/Marc Tulane; 41 below Christoph Kicherer; 42–43 Agence Top/Robert Cesar; 44–47 Paul Rocheleau; 48–53 Ray Main/Mainstream; 54–57 Vitra Design Museum, Weil am Rhein; 58 Harry Seidler & Associates; 59 above Arcaid/Richard Bryant; 59 below Vogue Living/Simon Kenny; 60–63 The Interior Archive/James Mortimer; 64–65 Strüwing Reklamefoto; 66 Julius Shulman; 67 Leif Wivelsted; 68 Julius Shulman; 69 Leif Wivelsted; 70–77 Graham Atkins Hughes; 78–83 Anders Overgaard; 84–91 Graham Atkins Hughes; 92 Arcaid/Scott Frances/ESTO; 93 left Arcaid/Richard Bryant; 93 right View/Peter Cook; 94–95 Photo © Lluís Casals; 96 Agence Top/Marc Tulane; 97 View/Peter Cook; 98 Tim Street-Porter; 99 The Bridgeman Art Library/Isokon Long Chair, designed for Isokon Furniture Company by Marcel Breuer; 100 The Interior Archive/Frtiz von der Schulenburg; 101 left The Interior Archive/Fritz von der Schulenburg; 101 right Iittala, Finland/Lasse Koivunen; 102 Tim Street-Porter; 103 left Tim Street-Porter; 103 right Herman Miller Inc. Photo Archives/Phil Schaafsma; 104 Tim Street-Porter/rocks placed by Noguchi; 105 Graham Atkins Hughes; 106 David Glomb; 107 Julius Shulman; 108 Taverne Agency/Mirjam Bleeker/Frank Visser; 109 Undine Pröhl; 110–11 Gio Ponti Photo Archive; 112 Laura Hodgson/designer Arne Jacobsen; 113 center Sotheby's Picture Library/Louis Poulsen; 113 left Laura Hodgson/designer Arne Jacobsen; 113 right Chameleon PR/Vola Products; 114 Verner Panton Design; 115 Vitra Design Museum, Weil am Rhein/Verner Panton Design; 116–17 Julius Shulman; 118–23 Trevor Mein; 124–29 Andrew Weaving; 130–41 Graham Atkins Hughes; 142–45 Andrew Wood; 146 Patrik Engquist; 147 above Åke E:son Lindman; 147 below Patrik Engquist; 148–49 Patrik Engquist; 150–53 Graham Atkins Hughes; 154–57 Martin Tessler; 158–63 Graham Atkins Hughes; 164–65 Michael Moran; 166–71 Graham Atkins Hughes; 172–73 Todd Hido/Light Waves; 174–79 David Glomb.